Y0-BVQ-718

MANAGING HUMAN SERVICES

JESSE F. McCLURE, EDITOR

Donated by Dean McClure, 198

INTERNATIONAL DIALOGUE PRESS · DAVIS · CALIFORNIA

Cover designs and illustrations for all
DIALOGUE BOOKS are created by the
well-known Swiss artist, Celestino Piatti

Library of Congress Card Number 79-66853
ISBN 0-89881-006-X

GILBERT HAMILTON, Research Director, Institute for Human Service Management, Sacramento, California

PETER HILL, Senior Socio-Economic Planner, Sacramento Regional Area Planning Commission, Sacramento, California

THOMAS P. HOLLAND, Chairman, Doctoral Program, School of Applied Social Sciences, Case Western Reserve University, Cleveland, Ohio

MITCHEL J. LAZARUS, Director of Planning and Budgeting, Minneapolis Federation for Jewish Services, Minnesota

MARY W. MACHT, Assistant Professor, School of Social Work, University of Wisconsin, Oshkosh

JAMES E. MILLS, Director, The Planning Council, Sacramento, California

ANN O'RIELLY, Consultant, Patrick Linnane and Associates, Boston, Massachusetts

JOSEPH O. PECENKA, College of Business, Northern Illinois University, DeKalb

FREDRICK W. SEIDL, Professor, School of Social Work, University of Wisconsin, Madison

ALLAN L. SERVICE, Consultant, Patrick Linnane and Associates, Boulder, Colorado

NEIL F. SHIFFLER, Department of Management, Bucknell University, Lewisburg, Pennsylvania

PETER F. SORENSEN, JR., Director of Graduate Studies, Organization Behavior and Administration, George Williams College, Downers Grove, Illinois

FRED THOMPSON, Associate Professor, Public and Not-For-Profit Management Program, Graduate School of Management, University of California, Los Angeles

TOINE VAN LUIJTELAAR, Controller, Ahold N.V., Zaandam, The
  Netherlands

ROBERT O. WASHINGTON, Dean, College of Social Work, Ohio State
  University, Columbus

MARION J. WOODS, Director, Department of Social Services, State of
  California

FOREWORD

In June 1978, residents of California passed a measure to reduce taxes, thus limiting revenues available for the administration of public institutions. Proposition 13 in California, and similar tax reduction measures in other states, have ushered in an era of budget limitations which have tested and will continue to test the imaginations of human service administrators.

The Institute for Human Service Management's first annual Conference, together with the present book reflecting and expanding on the Conference theme, represent to me a healthy sign that Proposition 13 will not lead to panic in the human services. Efforts are being made to examine ways in which high quality services can continue to be delivered despite cutbacks in funding at city and county levels. In California we clearly have no choice but to begin thinking about innovative ways to administer the state's multibillion-dollar-a-year human service programs.

California has constantly struggled to make its human service delivery system more efficient and effective. With Aid to Families with Dependent Children payments, no other large industrialized state has a lower dollar-error rate. Nevertheless, regardless of how efficient California is, because of limited tax revenues its record must become even better.

It is with the knowledge that disgruntled taxpayers across the country are placing tax reduction measures on their ballots — indicating they are no longer willing to support inefficient and ineffective human service programs — that I urge concerned citizens and workers in the human services to address the issues raised in this collection. It speaks to the great challenge of the future: to provide needed services in more efficient and imaginative ways.

> Marion J. Woods
> Director, Department of
> Social Services
> State of California

ACKNOWLEDGMENTS

Whenever one pursues the task of transforming a dynamic activity such as a conference into a more static medium such as a book, major problems emerge. Excellent oral presentations often are different in style from excellent written papers. In addition, papers presented in a conference setting, where individuals from many backgrounds have come together to share ideas, may suffer a loss of impact when transferred to the printed page. Finally, since even a brief three-day conference often will generate materials too voluminous to be published in their entirety in book form, difficult editorial decisions have to be made regarding selection of papers.

As we took on the task of producing this volume, each of these problems arose, as well as others too complex to describe here. Overriding these problems, however, was the need to have a written record of a most exciting event which occurred in June 1978. Despite its imperfections, this record has value in that it sets down some of our thoughts, opinions, and hopes at a particular point in time and allows us to measure our progress in understanding and acting in the future. Moreover, this volume contains a variety of approaches and solutions to problems which many of us face in our professional lives. I am sure that its readers too will find this a worthwhile effort.

To the participants and presenters at the conference I extend my thanks for the opportunity to have shared the experience. Our publisher, Ernst Wenk, was the energy source for this volume and made our hope a reality. With encouragement and persistence, the publication director of the Institute for Human Service Management, Louise Munro Foley, made sure that this volume was produced. To her and to other members of the Institute staff, especially Sylvia Cheng and Sharon Terry, I express my sincerest gratitude.

A special word of thanks is due to Diane Killou and Suzanne Mikesell for their editorial labors. The task, though massive, was accomplished with efficiency, competence, and good spirit.

Finally, I express my gratitude to my wife, Alnita T. McClure. Without her sound advice and counsel, little that I have done would have been possible.

PREFACE

The collection of writings in this volume is a result of the first annual Conference of the Institute for Human Service Management, held in Sacramento, California, June 28-30, 1978. The purpose of the Conference was to bring together knowledgeable persons from the business, academic, and human service communities to explore the state of the art of human service management. A call for papers was made nationally within these three groups.

Our primary intention was to begin a dialogue on the improvement of management in the human services through concentration on the problem of product. It is hoped that this dialogue will lead to the refined application of management technology in human service organizations. We do not pretend that we have exhausted the range of issues which could be developed in this area; the Institute's second annual Conference in 1980 will provide the occasion for more in-depth analyses. What we have done is to look at some of these concerns from a non-means orientation — that is, from an outcome perspective rather than a methods perspective. We are presenting these papers to human service managers, practitioners, and students, as well as other interested individuals, to remind us all that the basic concern in a human service organization should be not the activities or dynamics of a service but its outcome or product.

Jesse F. McClure

CONTENTS

INTRODUCTION:
THE PROBLEM OF PRODUCT

Jesse F. McClure

Human service organizations are a major component of American society. As our society has become more complex, these organizations and their programs have taken over many of the functions which were previously performed by families, neighborhoods, and communities. Because they are primarily governmental, human service organizations tend to increase in number in direct relationship to the growth of government. They now consume the bulk of government expenditure at all levels.

Accompanying this multiplication of human service organizations has been the growing recognition of the vast problems associated with their functioning. Many critics claim that human services are distributed inequitably and, more important, fail to produce meaningful changes in their clients' lives. At the same time as costs have escalated, numerous accounts of scandals in money management, program services, and licensing have been revealed. These problems combined have produced a crisis in the human service sector. Public concern about effectiveness of service and escalating costs has stimulated the development of two major stances toward resolving this crisis: one, that human service management should become more efficient and the other, that funding in the human services should be increased.

CONCERN FOR EFFICIENCY

Both practitioners and the general public have suggested that the human services need a large dose of business management practice. Those who adhere to this view maintain that the same techniques, programs, and policies which have made possible the development of one of the world's most advanced economic systems can also make possible a responsive, responsible, and efficient system of meeting human needs. They suggest that issues of productivity and effectiveness must be examined in the same way in the human services as in business, in terms of cost and profitability. Proponents of the infusion of business ideology into the human services system maintain that the use of business methods will result not only in less costly services but also in increased capabilities to meet genuine human needs. This approach has gained popularity with the public because of the growing disaffection with government in general and with increasing expenditure of tax funds for human services in particular. The result has been heated debates among politicians over reduction of spending and professionalization of management for these services.

This viewpoint is reflected in the public opinion polls of the 1970s. For example, a Harris poll on welfare conducted in June 1976 concluded that ". . . fundamentally the people are ambivalent about welfare. They have compassion for the less privileged, but they are also deeply disturbed by the operation of the welfare system." Ninety-four percent of the respondents said that it was not right for people who needed welfare to go hungry, and seventy-four percent said that many women whose husbands had left them with several children had no choice but to go on welfare. However, the same respondents were also very critical of welfare programs and eighty-nine percent said that too many people on welfare could be working, while eighty-five percent said that too many people on welfare cheated by getting money to which they were not entitled. Sixty-four percent said that the criteria for obtaining welfare were not stringent enough.

This survey found, however, that when it came to alleviating such problems, people did not want to change the system much at all. An overwhelming seventy-seven percent rejected the idea of giving people on welfare their money directly without red tape, but they felt also that at least a third of the funds being expended on welfare services could have been cut back without a serious loss in effectiveness. This group of people felt that inefficiency, rather than the nature of the welfare system itself, justified fund-cutting of such magnitude.

CONCERN FOR ADEQUATE FUNDING

The other stance that has emerged from this crisis in the human services has come primarily from professionals in the field and from the community of human service constituents. These people feel that the problems of human service programs are caused not by poor management but by inadequacy of funding, resulting from the ever-increasing demands for budget cuts. This group believes that the public's lack of understanding of programs also contributes to the current crisis. It is maintained that human service organizations cannot function like business organizations because their products are intangible and cannot be measured.

Proponents of this view argue that an infusion of business techniques would not necessarily produce either a more effective or a more efficient human service system. Societal dynamics, including political and cultural changes, impinge on service effectiveness. Social transformations such as those brought about by the civil rights movement and the movement for women's equality all have a bearing on the effectiveness of human service programs.

SPECIAL CHARACTER OF
HUMAN SERVICE ORGANIZATIONS

It is apparent that human service organizations are indeed different from those of traditional American enterprise and confront complex and unique problems. The gross application of business management practice has not led, and probably never will lead, to improved performance in the human services. What is needed is a more refined approach that takes into account the special character of the human service organization. There are a variety of tasks to be performed in the human service organization that are basically the same as tasks that must be performed in any other organization. These tasks include delivering financial reports and developing money management approaches, personnel practices, and general office procedures. We will call these the *uniform* aspects of human service delivery.

There is another dimension of the human service organization, however, which is not as responsive to business management techniques. Tasks associated with this dimension, termed *non-uniform* aspects of human service delivery, are the various processes, unique to human service delivery, which must be exercised to serve clients. These tasks exist because in order to provide human benefits a human service organization must have the capability to take into account the uniqueness of each individual being served.

A NEW APPROACH

By increasing the clarity of goals and objectives, the refined application of management technology proposed here can have a significant impact on *both* uniform and non-uniform activities of human service organizations. It will stimulate a greater emphasis on outcomes of these activities while decreasing the emphasis on the activities themselves. In this way the goals of both managers and practitioners can be brought together.

Traditionally, human service practitioners have been concerned with methods and techniques: in dealing with mental health problems, for example, the focus has been on what counseling techniques to use rather than on alternative desirable outcomes in a client's situation. The profession has been slow to develop common approaches to similar kinds of problems experienced by clients. For too long, it has concentrated on the individuality of the people served rather than on standardized strategies for identifying casework objectives and measuring results in terms of these objectives.

Just as human service professionals have been involved in technologies of counseling, human service managers have been involved in management processes — budgeting, planning, and evaluation techniques — often losing sight of the special problems and needs of caseworkers and their clients. It is important to remember that management is a process. It is a method, or a means to an end, and not an end in itself. Service techniques also are methods. When dealing with both, focus must be placed on outcomes.

It is suggested here that management practices can be applied with positive results even in the non-uniform areas of the human services. A human service organization must not only develop an adequate budget, mechanisms for handling personnel, and processes for planning and evaluating results, but must also take into consideration the specific needs of the clientele it serves. Thus the principal concern of the human services should not be efficiency (although efficiency is, of course, important); it should be the product.

The focus of the present collection of readings is on the product of human services — product being the end result, the *raison d'être* of the organization itself. What is the organization set up to achieve? What are the desired outcomes? These objectives must be stated in measurable terms so that at the end of a given period of time, or perhaps of a specific set of treatments or services, it can be determined whether the desired outcome has been achieved. In essence, the problem of product is the problem of accountability: given the current period of budget limitations resulting from Proposition 13 and other tax-reduction measures, how can human service organizations continue to provide needed services, yet also be accountable to the general public in terms of cost efficiency?

By focusing on product, managers and practitioners can work together to achieve accountability. Managers must learn to adapt management principles to the special conditions of human service delivery; practitioners must learn to adapt their professional activities to sound management principles. This book hopes to facilitate a dialogue between managers and practitioners by helping them to see that their goals are the same.

PART I

HUMAN SERVICE PLANNING

Management in the human services involves a complex set of tasks. In part, this complexity is due to the intangibility of human service products such as values, attitudes, and senses of well-being. The tasks of the human service manager are complicated also by the nature of management itself. While many definitions of management exist, the view in this volume is that management is the art and science of achieving goals by utilizing resources. The manager must use a process to produce a product.

From this definition it is apparent that management has an indirect rather than a direct relationship to the final product. Managing well and performing direct tasks well are separate skills. A great orchestra conductor, for example, is not necessarily a great artist when confined to playing one instrument. Similarly, an outstanding athlete does not necessarily become a successful coach. This is an especially important issue in the human services since most managers in this area are practitioners before moving into the management role. Too often this change of role occurs with little preparation for managing.

Implicit in the definition of management is that the first responsibility of managers is goal setting, which involves the process of planning. The authors in this section of the book are concerned with a number of views of human service planning.

O'Rielly and Service provide an organizational context in which planning occurs. Understanding of organizational goals and personal roles is a critical factor in reducing the problems associated with planning and management. Open communication is also a prerequisite to effective management.

Looking at human service planning from an operational perspective, Mills sees it in a highly political context. Instead of avoiding political realities, in Mills' view the human services must respond effectively to their challenges.

From the perspective of his experiences with the reorganization of human services in San Diego County, California, Caulk undertakes an analysis of human service planning. Like Mills, Caulk sees the need for effective responses in a politically charged atmosphere. From this case analysis he concludes that the fragmentation of human service activities need not continue.

Using another example, Hill approaches the problems of human service planning from the perspective of increasing coordination among existing programs and services rather than creating new structures or programs. Hill sees fragmentation in the human services as the result of the piecemeal development of most human service programs. Coordination is shown to be both desirable and feasible.

Finally, Hamilton presents some concrete techniques which can be employed to improve planning in the human services. PERT and the Critical Path Method are potentially important techniques for converting some of the "unknowns" in the human services to information that can be utilized to improve service delivery.

REDUCING INHIBITORS TO EFFECTIVE HUMAN SERVICE MANAGEMENT

Allan L. Service
Ann O'Rielly

This paper examines some aspects of current management practice in human service organizations and suggests some strategies which may improve that practice. The theme of the paper is that human service organizations and the people in them exhibit certain characteristics which are at least inhibitors and at most completely antithetical to effective management. The manager of a human service organization should recognize and understand these characteristics and accept the likelihood of their continued existence. The imaginative human service manager does not retreat into self-serving arguments that such characteristics do not or should not exist, but instead regards them as challenges to be overcome.

The paper is divided into four sections. The first is a brief discussion of the nature of management and the kinds of tasks managers are expected to carry out. The second section identifies several environmental or structural inhibitors to effective management, while the third section describes a parallel set of attitudinal inhibitors. The final section suggests some strategies which may be useful in reducing the impact of these inhibitors, thereby improving management practice in human service organizations.

THE NATURE OF MANAGEMENT

Many different models and definitions of management are available from published literature and experience. One of the earliest schools of thought concerning management was the *universalist* or *generalist* perspective developed by Henri Fayol[1] and others. This point of view holds that management is essentially the same in all organizations, and encompasses five basic elements: planning, organizing, commanding, coordinating, and controlling. The universalists were the first to view management as generic rather than as specific to the organization or context in which it is exercised.

A second major influential trend of management thought was the *scientific management* movement led by Frederick Taylor and his associates.[2] Scientific management argues that productivity will be maximized if each element of the organization's work is performed as efficiently as possible. The manager's task is to ensure this efficiency in individual tasks. Time and motion studies and other similarly detail-oriented activities are representative of the attitudes of the scientific management school.

In contrast to scientific management, which focuses on the tasks of workers, the *behavioral* or *human relations* approach regards relationships between and among people as keys to effective organizations. This school of thought first crystallized around Elton Mayo and the now classic Hawthorne studies.[3] The behaviorists regard the manager's major task as that of creating an environment which fosters and maintains effective interpersonal relationships. They argue that if the manager is successful in this task, organizational effectiveness will be a natural consequence.

The *operations research* or *systems analysis* approach to management first began to emerge during the latter stages of World War II. This field focuses on modeling, usually quantitatively, the decision problems faced by managers and on finding the most effective choice among a set of decisional alternatives. The work of C. West Churchman[4] and others emphasizes the need to understand as completely as possible the expected consequences of such managerial decisions. An offshoot of systems analysis is the *management systems* approach, which has had a variety of labels at different points in history including: Program Planning and Budgeting Systems (PPBS), Management by Objectives (MBO), and the currently fashionable Zero-Based Budgeting (ZBB). Although the specific steps and techniques used in these various approaches differ, all such systems share a certain logic. They are multistep packages intended to provide a framework for all aspects of management decision making, from goal setting to evaluation and feedback.

In practice, the effective manager does not follow any of these models exclusively. Rather, he or she draws from a complicated mix of these different schools of thought. Thus, for example, concerns of efficiency found in scientific management and concerns of effectiveness emphasized by systems analysis are combined with a complex set of concerns about human relations and behavioral factors. The manager draws also from his or her personal values, skills, and experiences. The dynamic and uncertain nature of organizations and the environment within which they exist adds a significant *ad hoc* component to management.

Because there are so many different perspectives, the task of developing a working definition of the nature of human service management can be risky. We therefore turn to a basic source, Webster's Dictionary, which

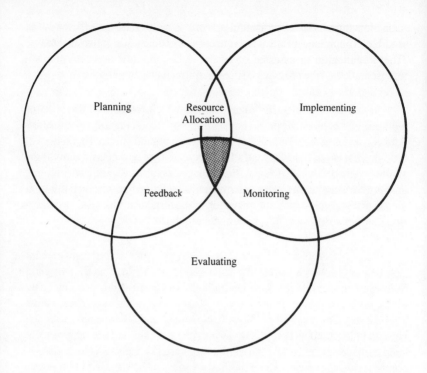

FIGURE 1
Management Tasks and Interrelationships

defines management as "the judicious use of means to accomplish an end." This simple definition identifies all of the key types of managerial tasks.

One set of tasks has a planning emphasis. The decisions involved are about future actions: defining desired ends, identifying resources needed and available to move toward those ends, and defining strategies and activities to apply these resources.

A second group of managerial tasks emphasizes the "judicious use" element of the management definition. The focus is on the present. Decisions are made about establishing and maintaining an internal organizational structure and a set of relationships with the external environment. Activities are carried out on a day-to-day basis and decisions are made as to whether these activities are conforming to a planned pattern.

Third, and perhaps most important, is the manager's responsibility for assessing the extent to which the desired ends have been accomplished.

Concerns here include the identification of intended and unintended results and the comparison of actual results with the desired ends earlier defined. These evaluation or assessment tasks are, for the most part, decisions or judgments about past activities. One of the key tasks of the manager is to establish the means whereby the assessment results can be utilized as feedback to the system, so that as the cycle continues appropriate changes can be made on the basis of experience.

The manager's task is a complex mix of planning, implementing, and evaluating activities. None of these functions is carried out in isolation. Rather there are extensive interactions between and among various functional and decision areas. Schematically, the situation may be represented as in Figure 1. All of the functions overlap and the manager's role lies at the center of this complex of interactions.

ENVIRONMENTAL INHIBITORS TO
EFFECTIVE HUMAN SERVICE MANAGEMENT

In the human services, the management tasks described are carried out in a complex environmental and social context. We argue that understanding the unique characteristics of this environment is a critical element in a human service manager's effectiveness. There seem to be five major inhibiting factors or groups of factors which he or she must understand.

One factor is that the fundamental building blocks of human service organizations are interactions between people. Any interaction between individuals is a complex and largely intangible process. When an entire organization is concerned with producing and changing such interactions, the resulting system is tremendously complicated. The situation is complicated further by the values, preferences, and characteristics of the individuals and groups involved. In addition, even single interactions have multiple purposes and roles. Furthermore, all of these internal human interactions are surrounded by a complex network of external organizations and constituencies which impinge upon and constrain an organization and its management.

A second group of inhibiting factors arises from the complex and intangible nature of goals and results that characterize human service organizations. There is no right answer; goals are a collection of value judgments, and an organization follows ends which, on the basis of individual and collective values, it regards as desirable at a given point in time. Since values differ across individuals, groups, and organizations, there may not be a real

23

consensus on these goals. Furthermore, human service organizations usually have multiple goals.

The measurement of success for any human service organization or its management is therefore a very ambiguous matter. It is further compounded by the difficulty of measuring a human service organization's results, which are mostly intangible and occur over long periods of time. There may not be agreement on what the results of an organization's efforts *are,* much less on whether these results are desirable. Human service organizations tend to rely on proxy measures of activity levels, efficiency, or indirect effects. This point is particularly relevant to management, since judgment of a manager's ability to move towards desired ends is severely curtailed by an inability to measure the extent to which the ends are reached. Thus, managerial effectiveness is often judged in inappropriate ways or not at all.

A third inhibitor is the indeterminate nature of the technology that characterizes most human service organizations. Most of this technology consists of direct interactions between individuals and produces the diverse and intangible results mentioned above. Clients themselves are inherently variable and unpredictable. Furthermore, current knowledge of cause and effect phenomena in the human services is severely limited. We know that certain kinds of outcomes occur, but have limited knowledge of *why* they occur. Thus, the manager's task of marshalling resources to most effectively move toward desired ends is undertaken with limited knowledge of the most effective way to deploy available resources.

The human service manager's job is further complicated by a fourth inhibitor, which is that of multiple and possibly conflicting demands for accountability. The general public, funding bodies, clients, staff, and ancillary organizations all have their own values and their own opinions as to what the product of the organization should be and how effectiveness should be documented. The manager is faced with the task of balancing the demands of these various groups.

The final kind of inhibitor is not confined to human service organizations but nevertheless merits attention. The size, diversity, and complexity of human service organizations make them inherently difficult to manage. They serve a wide range of clients and provide a variety of services. Substantial resource commitments and diverse professional staffs are often involved. Complex organizational patterns involving decentralization, coordination of services, and multiple funding sources also characterize many human service organizations. The net result is that the organizations are difficult to even understand, much less manage in a consistent fashion. These difficulties and the challenges they represent are a fact of life for human service managers.

ATTITUDINAL INHIBITORS TO EFFECTIVE HUMAN SERVICE MANAGEMENT

There are other inhibitors to effective management which are often overlooked or even deliberately denied because of the discomfort associated with them. Grouped under the heading of attitudinal inhibitors, these include value judgments, biases, and prevailing opinions and can make the human service manager's job more difficult, particularly if he is unaware of them or chooses to deny them. Whether such attitudes are correct or incorrect — indeed, we take exception to many of them — is not the issue. These attitudes do exist and must be reckoned with. While not an exhaustive list, the following attitudes seem representative of attitudinal inhibitors to effective management.

"Human service organizations are relatively simple and managing them is easy." Despite the existence of many environmental inhibitors, there is a substantial body of opinion that appears not to recognize the inherent complexity of human service organizations and of the effects they attempt to produce. This attitude is fostered in part by memories of earlier times when human service organizations were smaller, often single purpose, and comparatively simple to manage. A trace of nostalgia for the "good old days" may be involved as well.

"Using resources for management detracts from the service delivery mission of human service organizations." There is no doubt that the fundamental purpose of human service organizations is to serve people by helping to improve their lives. When this focus is coupled with the difficulty of articulating the direct contribution of management to effective service delivery, the attitude that the use of resources for management detracts from service delivery capability is easy to predict. Management is a support activity and fully understanding its contribution may require a leap of faith. Skepticism about the contribution is increased by the sometimes overstated claims of managers and those who purport to assist them with systems or other kinds of technology. "Better" management has been presented in some circles as an answer to all human service problems. When the answer fails to materialize, a negative attitude toward management and managers often emerges.

"Management leads to bureaucracy and stagnation." The undeniable existence of poor management in some human service organizations, coupled with all of the environmental inhibitors identified above, almost inevitably gives rise to this attitude. It is easy to conclude from looking at large and inefficient human service systems that management is part of the reason for the emergence of bureaucracies. While it is probably not possible to prove that this attitude is incorrect, its fairly widespread existence must be recognized.

"Management requires no special skills; anyone can be a manager." The origin of this attitude is easy to see. Most human service managers begin as direct service practitioners and progress upward in an organization until they become managers. However, while they are labeled managers, they may have no particular training or even skills in management, although they may be expert clinicians or direct service providers. The fact that they, nevertheless, function as managers lends credence to the attitude that management is a marginal or intuitive activity. This attitude reinforces some of the other negative attitudes toward management discussed above. It also works against efforts to improve management training for human service organizations and to understand how to manage human service organizations effectively.

"The use of management techniques is threatening because it makes decisions and their implications more visible." Although seldom clearly articulated, this is a real fear for many individuals. Better management does not necessarily mean easier or less threatening management. The manager who can argue "I had no other choice" has effectively avoided many of the negative possibilities associated with accountability. On the other hand, if a manager sets forth alternatives and some of their expected consequences, there is a much more sound and often more visible basis for evaluating his achievements. Taking risks is difficult, and when the payoffs associated with effective management are vague and ambiguous, it is not surprising that many resist attempts to improve management, believing it will make their jobs more difficult and more risky.

STRATEGIES FOR REDUCING INHIBITORS TO EFFECTIVE HUMAN SERVICE MANAGEMENT

Clearly, the human service manager is confronted with a Herculean task. Management itself is a complex activity involving a dynamic set of interrelated tasks. The environmental and attitudinal inhibitors to effective management in human service organizations make the job of managers there even more challenging. Having identified some of these inhibitors, we now suggest some strategies which may be useful in overcoming them and in improving management practice in human service organizations.

It seems essential that the manager who wishes to upgrade the quality of management in a human service organization first assess the capacity and willingness of the organization's members to engage in change activities. Almost anything can be changed, but the amount of difficulty associated with accomplishing change is directly related to the willingness to cooperate of those involved in or affected by the change.

The manager's first task therefore is to establish a climate of trust within the organization. The essential element in this climate of trust is accessibility. Managerial isolation thwarts positive change by prohibiting the establishment of trust. A manager must be readily available to the staff and willing to devote the time and energy necessary to develop a mutual sense of trust. Effective two-way communication is essential, since a manager must know the experience and perceptions of the staff and the staff must know the manager and his concerns. When this sharing occurs, some of the mystique surrounding management is dispelled. The channels of communication which are developed will be critical to the implementation of new practices in the organization.

A second strategy for reducing the friction between management techniques and the human service organization is to develop and articulate a clear and shared sense of organizational mission. This step is a prerequisite to engaging staff in change. If management is to be successful, both the manager and his staff must understand why the organization exists and to what ends its activities are directed. The goals and objectives of the organization as well as the tasks assigned to the staff are derived from the mission. When a shared sense of organizational mission is achieved, staff can see how their role is related to the overall purpose of the organization and how management supports and links the two.

Pursuing this line, we come to a third strategy: to delineate decision-making and management roles of individuals at all organizational levels. Management functions are not limited to the top administrative levels of an organization, but occur at every level. The effective manager must help each individual to understand the part he or she plays in the management of the organization. The identification of those aspects of a person's responsibilities which are management activities has two important consequences: (1) It suggests to all members of the organizational team that they contribute to the achievement of the organizational goals. (2) It makes management real to everyone concerned.

A fourth strategy calls upon the manager to acknowledge that management, particularly in the human services, is a supportive rather than a directive activity. Good management should provide a framework by which organizational activities can be structured and coordinated to achieve optimal resource utilization in pursuit of the organization's goals. If the management of the organization is decentralized enough so that each individual perceives that he or she has a part to play in its operation, management will flow upward through the organization. Management which originates in the workings of the organization has a much better prognosis than management which issues decisions, policies, and procedures from behind closed doors. A management network can be seen to support and augment the efforts of the staff. Good management has many resources to offer the human service organization, and the skilled manager who avoids a directive style can guide the organization in the use of these resources.

A final strategy for reducing the inhibitors to effective management in the human services requires some risk taking and does not guarantee positive results. This strategy involves a policy of openly examining the costs and benefits of managerial activities. This process exposes management practices to scrutiny and, undoubtedly, to criticism. However, it also means that when the utilization of a management technique has a benefit, this, too, is visible to the organization. Only when gains are documented will management be able to build a constituency in the human services. Open acknowledgment of the costs — time and money — involved in introducing new management approaches into an organization can go a long way toward reducing the attitudinal resistance to innovation. Management is not the answer to all human service problems. It does, however, have a critical role to play in the improvement of the operation of human service organizations. The enterprising and imaginative human service manager must clearly point out not only the contribution that management can make but also the effort necessary to make that contribution a reality.

One other point should be made. All of the strategies suggested here are essentially short-term and oriented toward the internal workings of individual organizations. A longer-term and more general strategy for reducing inhibitors to effective management is to promote the education and training of cadres of managers specifically for human service organizations. Until and unless individuals knowledgeable about *both* management *and* the uniqueness of human service organizations are available, many of the inhibitors outlined in this paper will persist.

FOOTNOTES

1. H. Fayol, *General and Industrial Management* (London: Pitman, 1949).

2. F. W. Taylor, *Principles of Scientific Management* (New York: Harper Bros., 1911).

3. E. Mayo, *The Human Problems of an Industrial Civilization* (Cambridge, Mass.: Harvard Graduate School of Business Administration, 1946).

4. C. W. Churchman, *The Systems Approach* (New York: Delacourt, 1978); C. W. Churchman, *The Design of Inquiring Systems: Basic Concepts of Systems and Organization* (New York: Basic Books, 1971).

REFERENCES

Brown, J. W., and Barton, L. J. "Development and Use of Management Information and Planning Systems in Higher Education." In *Higher Education Information Systems: The Challenge of Change*. Edited by Jane N. Ryland and Charles R. Thomas. Boulder: College and University Systems Exchange, 1975.

Churchman, C. W. *The Systems Approach*. New York: Delacourt, 1978.

Churchman, C. W. *The Design of Inquiring Systems: Basic Concepts of Systems and Organization*. New York: Basic Books, 1971.

Fayol, H. *General and Industrial Management*. London: Pitman, 1949.

Hasenfeld, Y., and English, R. A. *Human Service Organizations*. Ann Arbor, Mich.: University of Michigan Press, 1974.

Mayo, E. *The Human Problems of an Industrial Civilization*. Cambridge, Mass.: Harvard Graduate School of Business Administration, 1946.

Taylor, F. W. *Principles of Scientific Management*. New York: Harper Bros., 1911.

HUMAN SERVICE PLANNING

James E. Mills

While the intrinsic value of human service planning is well recognized — particularly by human service planners — we have become painfully aware of the obstacles to good planning and, more important, to the implementing of plans. Human service planning suffers from the lack of a national social policy. Without a national policy (something more specific than the Declaration of Independence and the Constitution) within which to plan, we are destined to repeat past mistakes and to know only intuitively whether we are even moving forward.

Efforts to achieve a national consensus on social goals are bound to collide with a range of moral judgments and values as broad as the nation itself. Planners are confronted with values that often are only a thin veneer upon totally different values, and "long-range" plans are often based on fads. Lacking a standard approach to planning, we have substituted the individualism of incompatible systems, which vary from program to program and from one state and major locality to another. We have no means (discounting the census) of systematically collecting nationwide social data and no accepted service definitions or units of measure to which such a data-collection system could be related.

It is understandable that, lacking national social goals, we lack also national leadership. With the possible exception of health planning, there are few meaningful attempts at the federal level to cope with the myriad human service plans which have been developed in response to a variety of personal and group goals and which, unfortunately, do not in their totality equal a national social policy. There is little if any effort to integrate programs or even to develop coordination mechanisms.

Much of the responsibility for the existence of this situation falls on a combination of special interest legislation, the bureaucracy that thrives on maintaining and/or expanding special interest programs, and the single-minded advocacy group. The net result is fiscal and programmatic anarchy: a maze of programs and services that puzzle the client, frustrate the professional, and more often than not outrage the taxpayer. (Of the three parties, the latter seems most ready to act to rectify the situation.) "Success" of a program depends on grantsmanship skills and on the ability to redefine an existing program to meet the priority of the moment. Private funding sources are no less guilty in their practices than public ones. Within this framework, categorical and sub-categorical programming — much of what is called human service planning — takes place. In truth, however, most of this "planning" is no more than fiscal justification of prior judgments on the allocation of resources.

This situation is justified by our national commitment to pluralism, which is a basic part of our democratic beliefs. Since the nation to date has been willing to assume its costs, there exists the widest possible range of service sponsorships, special interest organizations, treatment modalities, and individual and group goals and objectives, all reasonably well tolerated by society. This commitment to pluralism is reinforced by a deep-seated resistance to "social engineering," a resistance which is very much a part of the national fiber and a constant threat to the concept of planning services for and with people.

Planning is plagued not only by the problem of pluralism but also by the related problem of capacity to change within a pluralistic setting. Too many of our human service agencies are small- or medium-sized, under-administered, and marginal in organizational vitality. Since they have limited "risk capital" to undertake new programs or remodel old ones, they have limited program planning and development capacity. An inordinate proportion of administrative resources is devoted to pure survival. In these settings, as well as in larger, more stable settings, planning and program development are in competition with direct services for resources. No matter how rational the argument may be that in a period of scarce resources adequate planning is more necessary than ever, resources will inevitably shift toward direct service delivery. These factors limit an agency's capacity to translate plans into programs.

Another basic American belief is that competition strengthens all parties concerned. In the field of human service planning there is little opportunity for this thesis to be effectively tested, since most of the resources for human services come from government sources. Because of the relationship between the recipient and the funding body, true competition will never emerge. The parallel system that might have offered competition (the United Way) has been systematically dismantling its community planning structure and substituting an operational planning system more directly related to the demands of its allocation process. Thus, competition should not be counted upon to be the factor that will bring human service planning into its own.

31

While the element of political decision making exists in the human services as in other areas, it is not as well accepted in the human services as it is in diplomacy, defense policy, or economic programming. It is in the human services that idealism and political compromise have their most stubborn confrontation. Political decision making has various aspects. One aspect is that of the planner's perennial problem of territoriality: conflicting professional disciplines, public sector versus private sector, pathological model versus health model, sectarian versus non-sectarian, and state versus county. These and other boundaries — real or artificial — contribute significantly to the fragmentation and stratification of people, their problems, and the programs designed to meet their needs.

Other aspects of political decision making are more closely related to the common meaning of the term — that is, politicians (not necessarily elected) making decisions. This process is essentially the same in human services as it is in other areas. There are the political decisions that reflect the will of the electorate — and until you have lived in a state with the power of the initiative, you may not realize just how precisely that will can be expressed! In this case, in making a decision a politician usually reflects what he perceives to be political reality. On the other hand, a political decision (whether in the judicial, legislative, or executive branch of government, the corporate board room, or the non-profit sector) can be tactical. In this case, the politician must decide, "What are the accommodations that must be made to achieve my goals or my organization's goals?" This process of accommodation is an accepted part of our democracy and has not been the primary focus of criticism in current challenges to social institutions and practices.

If human service planning is seen as a political process in a democratic society, it is possible to develop a conceptualization that is workable and productive in spite of the noted limitations. Despite the hostile environment in which human service planning takes place, it is possible to develop a concept of "politicized human service planning" that need not require the abandonment of either ethics or the emerging technology of planning.

If politics is the practice of the art of the possible, what steps can be taken to make the products of the planning process more realizable? Each planner is motivated by a high degree of idealism, but the most "successful" planners have been those who have been able to resist the temptation to impose their ideals wholesale on others. They have not forsaken their ideals but have adopted a policy of incrementalism. When steadily applied with clear goals in mind, incrementalism results in consistent movement toward major change which would be rejected outright if proposed in a single step. A narrower scope, a longer-range strategy, or a less comprehensive plan has greater political viability and thus a greater chance of being implemented.

Since change is threatening to individuals and organizations alike, a plan must contain incentives if steps toward necessary change are to be undertaken. There must be a "pay off" for each major element involved. Therefore, the design of an effective plan must emphasize implementation strategies. As in many phases of the human services, greater attention must be paid to treatment, not at the expense of diagnosis but as the natural end product and only logical justification for diagnosis.

Since such words as "integrated" and "comprehensive" are not yet part of the national consciousness, planning efforts should be focused on coordination rather than integration of services. There is little support for meaningful coordination and even less for integration. While integration experiments are important and should continue, the feasibility of the integration of services cannot yet be demonstrated. Until the results of integration efforts are known and their transferability assessed, a much more realistic approach is to develop better mechanisms for service coordination. In addition to having a higher degree of political acceptability, successful coordination experiences can lay a strong foundation for later integration efforts.

Plans must be developed allowing decision makers a degree of discretion, while at the same time limiting the range of "political dealing." These conditions can be met if plans have a maximum degree of rationality and if increasingly irrational political choices demand of the decision maker increasing public justification.

A highly political conceptualization of human service planning suggests many potential moral and ethical dilemmas. It calls for mature planners, skilled in their craft and acutely aware of their ethical commitments to their profession and to the community. If human service planning is recognized as a political process, legitimate accommodations can be identified and built into the planning process to improve a plan's chances for eventual acceptance and implementation.

SOME PRINCIPLES FOR
HUMAN SERVICES REORGANIZATION

Robert S. Caulk

In May 1976, the County of San Diego Board of Supervisors adopted the Human Resources Agency Reorganization Plan. This Plan was the cornerstone for the creation of the Department of Human Services, which consolidated five separate programs (Area Agency on Aging, Department of Special Manpower Services, Human Care Services Program, Community Action Program, and Project 86) into one integrated functional administrative structure. More importantly, the Plan outlined a phased process which began in July 1977. This process was designed to provide the information base necessary to further reorganize human service activities along functional lines for greater integration, rationality, and economy in service provision. The assumption behind the Plan was that, in accordance with categorical mandates, parallel activities were occurring whose categorical structures could be disintegrated only after lengthy review, preparation of waivers, and other bureaucratic activity.

The passage of Proposition 13 has rendered some of these assumptions obsolete. Further, the demand for economy, efficiency, and understandable programs is so great that the opportunity exists for accelerated change toward a more effective, systematic, and humane approach. The County of San Diego has assumed national leadership in human service planning during the past five years. In spite of the apparent adversity presented by Proposition 13, it is highly appropriate that such leadership should continue.

The purpose of this paper is to develop a framework for the creation of a new direction in human service delivery in San Diego County. A few of the salient organizational and conceptual issues which apply to the development of the County's human services system will be presented. This presentation is not assumed to be exhaustive, but will review some of the matters which should be addressed when reorganization of structure is considered.

ORGANIZATIONAL PRINCIPLES

Phased Implementation

One of the variables in the success or failure of reorganization of complex structures is timing. If reorganization is begun prior to the establishment of goals and objectives, the new structures probably will fail to satisfy anyone's expectations and will quickly be replaced. The creation of the California State Department of Health is a clear example of how reorganization based on fallacious premises and unsound economics is doomed to failure. Conversely, the County of San Diego Human Resources Agency Reorganization Plan included provisions for analysis prior to the implementation of structural change. To maximize the possibilities of "success," this phased process allowed for systematic planning, adjustment for changing circumstances, and flexibility in design. Thus, the first principle of reorganization is that an incremental (phased) timetable should be established, with reasonable benchmarks providing adequate time to examine complex policy, procedural, and structural concerns.

Purchase vs. Provision

A second organizational issue which should be resolved at the outset pertains to the distinction between management of the *purchase* of services (primarily through contracts) and management of the *provision* of services (through delivery programs using County staff). In recent years, local governments have had to resolve the dilemma of how to meet increasing demands for specialized human services in the face of equally vociferous demands for a reduction in the size of government. Since 1973, the County of San Diego has addressed this dilemma by expanding the purchase of human services through contracts rather than by expanding the number of County employees to provide services directly. If administered carefully, the purchase of services can help reduce costs as well as simplify and rationalize human service delivery by linking private, nonprofit, community-based agencies to the larger service structures such as those of welfare, probation, mental health, and others.

In terms of administration and program management, the activities associated with purchase arrangements (requests for proposals, standardized contracts, scopes of services, contract management, monitoring and evaluation, fiscal control, community input, etc.) are dramatically different from those associated with the direct provision of service (licensing and credentials, case record systems, client intervention strategies, overcoming barriers to services, etc.). If this assumption of differences is correct, reorganization should reflect the clear separation of purchase from provision. This separation does not mean that service program concerns (such as content and method) should be ignored by contracting departments or vice versa. Instead, technical assistance on delivery issues should be available from the delivery structure while expertise in such areas as program structure and accountability should be available from the contracting department.

35

Fracturing

A third organizational issue is the most important if any improvements are to be achieved through reorganization. One cannot expect to obtain improvements simply by shifting existing departments and programs to different jurisdictions. Because such reorganization is often substituted for substantive policy and delivery changes and obscures the fundamental issues, these changes may in fact cause costs to increase and services to deteriorate.

To avoid this problem, the concept of "fracturing" must be introduced: that is, instead of realigning program elements along categorical lines, current structures (departments) are "fractured" and their components redistributed. It may no longer be appropriate to include certain activities in the jurisdictions where they have traditionally been placed. It might be more efficient and effective to centralize the management of human service institutions so that, for example, institutional matters such as the purchase of meal service are located in one place while programming is in another. Again, the purchase of service through contracts, vouchers, or other arrangements might be located in one department, while direct delivery of service remains in another. The point is that while wholesale shifts of departments under an umbrella agency do not guarantee real change, realignment of functional components outside traditional or categorical boundaries holds greater promise.

CONCEPTUAL PRINCIPLES

Functional vs. Categorical

Beyond the more mundane organizational issues, there are many conceptual issues pertaining to the delivery of human services by local governments. Only a few of the salient issues will be presented here. The first involves the choice between delivery of service along categorical lines and integration of service along functional lines. There is a wide range of assumptions and issues surrounding the concept of "integration of services" alone. Such questions as whether integration is a goal or a process, or whether it can best be achieved by co-location, case management, professional case consultation, administration, or policy, will not be addressed here. It is important, however, to point out that there is tremendous pressure to organize services along the categorical lines established by federal and state laws, regulations, and agencies. This pressure includes very clear fiscal incentives involving the level of federal matching funds and methods of cost accounting for the amount of overhead that can be claimed. It includes also a variety of program compliance regulations — which may or may not pertain to the delivery of quality services — such as the structure and role of advisory boards, eligibility determination, and the creation of annual program plans. While any one set of fiscal and program regulations might provide reasonable guidelines for administration, each categorical program has a discrete set which must be dealt with separately.

However, Proposition 13 can be interpreted as meaning that the public is ready for "straight talk" on human service delivery and that maintenance of parallel structures and adherence to detailed bureaucratic regulations (which may or may not reflect the intent of legislation) are no longer necessary. Instead, the duplication and confusion inherent in current arrangements can be replaced by creative reorganization according to management and service functions. If this reorganization is to occur, we must answer such basic questions as: who is to be served? to what ends? at what cost? and through what structures?

Thus it is apparent that, since structural form follows the logical arrangement of similar functions, the question of appropriateness of organizational structure should be considered last. When form follows function, benefits such as efficiency and orderliness are more likely to result. However, a realistic appraisal of constraints imposed by grantors at the state and federal levels should be conducted so that proper waivers can be prepared and so that acceptable cost accounting practices can be established. In short, the principle of fracturing departments and programs along functional lines appears to hold greater promise than does categorical division. While much effort has been expended in the past five years toward the achievement of functional integration, the "taxpayer revolt" may provide an additional opportunity for substantive change.

Three-Tiered Model

A second conceptual issue pertains to the distribution of services and to delivery structures. Basically, we must begin to determine which services are most appropriate at the community level, which at the regional level, and which should be delivered centrally. The choices inherent in this issue involve consideration of such factors as level of demand for certain services, assurance of access, and level of technology involved in the service. For example, child care should be provided at the local level, while certain residential treatment facilities might best be located regionally. Adoption services could be adequately delivered from a central location. The demand for child care is great, access is best in neighborhoods (where the service can be most sensitive to racial and cultural imperatives), and the service does not require investments in complex technology. Adoptions, conversely, involve a relatively limited demand, and persons interested in adopting a child usually can afford transportation to a central location where the somewhat complicated legal and social activities can occur.

The same three-tiered model can be applied to services involving health care. Ambulatory care, well-baby clinics, family planning, immunizations, prevention and education, information and referral, and similar services should be locally based. Comprehensive care for outpatients, X-ray and higher technologies, dental care, psychiatric screening, and the like should be provided regionally. Inpatient care involving the highest technology (scanners, dialysis, etc.) and other secondary care, as well as tertiary services involving specialized care such as for burns and certain traumas, should be centralized.

The three-tiered model can be used as a guide for appropriately locating most services, including both those that are purchased and those that are provided. Services that are presently provided by County staff can be sorted in this manner, with workers placed in community-based settings, in regional offices, or in a county center. A combination of the three tiers should assure both economies of scale and sensitivity to the diverse demography and topography of the County.

Purchase vs. Provision

A third conceptual issue involves how to distinguish between which services should be purchased (and therefore provided under the auspices of private nonprofit and proprietary agencies) and which services should be the exclusive domain of the County. This issue has been festering for the past five years with the emergence of broad-based contracting. In the juvenile justice field, for example, a number of probation department activities and clients have shifted to contractors, especially since the passage of a bill which provides for the deinstitutionalization of youth involved in status offenses.[1] However, there is legitimate concern about the ability of community-based agencies to serve youth who are not merely status offenders but who have performed overt criminal acts against persons or property.[2]

38

The issue can be resolved if we delegate to the County those services which involve primarily social control and community protection, while we allow prevention and social enhancement (including rehabilitation) services to be purchased. In this way, the probation officer or social worker retains the authority for supervising a delinquent youth or removing an abused child from a dangerous home. Such activities involve legally mandated and court related actions, which should remain under government jurisdiction. Other services, such as reuniting a runaway youth with his family, or diverting children and youth from further contact with the juvenile justice system by establishing alternative activities, attitudes, and group involvement, may best be provided by community-based agencies.

SUMMARY

The previous pages have discussed a number of organizational and conceptual principles for creating a more effective and efficient human service structure. The organizational principles include: the development of an incremental (phased) timetable for analysis, planning, and implementation; the creation of management structures in a way which differentiates between those devoted to the purchase of service and those providing services; and the fracturing of present departments (and even programs) where necessary instead of simply shifting them intact from one jurisdiction to another.

The conceptual principles include: the need to reorganize all County human services along functional lines rather than to continue the parallel structures created by categorical programming; the dispensing of services in accordance with a three-tiered model of local, regional, and centralized delivery; and the continuation in the public sector of services which involve social control and community protection. The intent of this paper has been to provide a step toward clarification of some of the points that deserve further attention as planning and reorganization continue.

FOOTNOTES

1. State of California, Statutes of 1976, AB 3121, Chapter 1071.
2. State of California, Welfare and Institutions Code, Section 602.

COORDINATION OF HUMAN SERVICES

Peter Hill

Coordination of human services is frequently discussed but seldom implemented. A large part of the problem is that there is no agreed upon definition of coordination. Views on what coordination is range from talking to another person in the human service field about a program to service integration.

From the perspective of a council of governments, the areas which are the most interesting and in which significant progress in coordination can be made are those of planning and funding. These areas have therefore been our targets in attempting to begin human service coordination in Sacramento.

During our attempts to achieve coordination, we have noted some key barriers which we feel cause local officials, policy makers, staffs of human service agencies, citizens, consumers, and taxpayers to be confused and often angry. These barriers often block efforts at starting coordination or destroy existing efforts. Barriers must be recognized and overcome if efforts toward coordination are to have positive results.

The key barriers we see are:

1. Historically, human service delivery systems have been developed using a piecemeal approach in response to the needs of the moment, to political pressure, and often to federal priorities and programs.

2. Human service funding is a highly political struggle; agencies seek and are granted funds from a variety of sources, their success seemingly limited only by their prowess in grantsmanship and, in some instances, their ability to resort to pressure tactics.

3. The proliferation of human service funding sources has fostered a confusing human service system composed of many independent sub-systems, each made up of agencies with narrow areas of interest.

4. Human service funding is authorized by a variety of legislative mandates, often with overlapping program responsibilities. Funding often is provided from federal, state, and local sources without coordination because each source is often unaware of the others' programs.

5. Since no agency or unit of government has assumed the responsibility for coordinating funding decisions, there is no coordination of local funding sources in their annual distribution of human service funding.

6. The variety of funding cycles and the timing of grants inhibit coordination of planning and funding efforts, and the annual funding confusion, compounded by the uncertainty of funding levels, makes long-range and cross-program planning extremely difficult.

7. There is no single source of comprehensive information about the programs operating in a local jurisdiction and their sources of funding.

8. There is no clearly identified point of coordination for human service planning.

9. There is no overall human service plan, combining goals and objectives, which guides funding to meet community needs and priorities. Each program responds to perceived needs in isolation and few, if any, attempts have been made to develop a comprehensive approach to meet the needs of the total person, family, or community through the social service delivery system.

10. There is minimal coordination of human service planning efforts among local government, the state, federal agencies, councils of government, and private sector voluntary agencies.

11. The complexity of the human service funding flow causes a lack of information about the organization of the human service system, and the multiplicity of funding sources and the overlap of federal, regional, and state involvement in most programs result in confusion concerning potential program interactions.

12. There is a lack of accountability in the human services because of the complexity of the human service delivery system and the failure to define roles and responsibilities.

Taken as a whole, these barriers form a dismal picture of the state of coordination in human service planning and funding. As a council of governments, we felt we should make an effort to call attention to these barriers and to propose some initial steps toward the coordination of planning and funding of human services.

Through some work we had done in initiating joint purchasing by senior citizen nutrition projects, we had discovered that funders and service providers were willing to cooperate in coordination efforts if they understood the problems and the benefits and if there were a leader acting as a catalyst. Our initial effort toward coordination of human service planning and funding was the preparation of a report entitled, "Human Service Funding, An Alternative Management Proposal."[1] This report was designed to provide information on human service funding controlled by local decisions. In fairly simple terms the report describes the extent of funds being allocated to human service programs, how funds flow into a jurisdiction, who was receiving the funds, the legislative mandate, and local administration of the funds. We have distributed over eight hundred copies nationwide.

Also included in the report were recommendations concerning the funding of human service programs. Four of the recommendations have played a key role in subsequent coordination activities undertaken in Sacramento:

1. Local governments should act as the focal point of human service planning by encouraging the various funding sources to use a partnership approach in meeting the priority needs of a community.

2. Funding sources should develop and use standardized application forms and should require that each applicant submit a full agency budget, including a full statement of all financial resources currently supporting its programs. Information regarding ongoing funding requests or negotiations in which the agency or contractor may be involved also should be provided.

3. Local jurisdictions should establish a centralized human service data and information system, including complete and up-to-date information on funding sources, timing of grants, local grantees, levels of funding, funding procedures, and program responsibilities in meeting community needs. Such information should be easily accessible to decision makers and to the general public.

4. Each local jurisdiction should establish a Human Service Funders Roundtable, bringing together all human service funding sources (including local government) that allocate funds to outside agencies for the provision of human services. The Human Service Funders Roundtable would provide the forum for the exchange of information, the coordination of funding decisions, and the joint planning and coordination of program operations.

Late in 1976, activities were undertaken by a group of human service planning and funding agencies in Sacramento to develop an integrated needs assessment. Although these efforts were unsuccessful, the participants continued discussions which led eventually to the establishment of the Sacramento Human Service Coordination Project and subsequently to the formation of the Human Service Funders Roundtable.

The Roundtable is made up of the following:

— Sacramento County
— Sacramento-Yolo Employment Training Agency
— Sacramento Area Economic Opportunity Council
— Area 4 Agency on Aging Community Service Planning Council
— Region D Criminal Justice and Juvenile Delinquency
— United Way of Sacramento
— Alta California Regional Center (for the developmentally disabled)
— City of Sacramento.

Support for the project is provided by Sacramento Regional Area Planning Commission staff, with myself as the Project Manager. The participating agencies have also supplied staff time to the project.

During the first year of the project, the following activities have been accomplished:

— Organization of Human Service Funders Roundtable
— Organization of Roundtable Advisory Committee made up of community-based service agencies
— Preparation of a Human Service Planning Calendar, which provides detailed information on planning events and timetable
— Preparation of a Human Service Funding Calendar, which provides detailed information on funding events and timetable
— Preparation of broad service-area definitions
— Identification and collection of existing human service plans
— Preparation of a Common Application Form for human service funding requests
— Preparation of a recommendation for a Common Funding Cycle.

Each of these activities has been the result of intensive discussion by the Roundtable and has not been without considerable controversy. The results, however, are encouraging. From a point, twelve months ago, when some members of the Roundtable did not know each other, they have progressed to the point of discussing how to implement such things as: a Common

Application Form for all funding agencies, a Common Funding Cycle, a joint advisory body review of program proposals, and coordinated funding decisions.

In addition, the Roundtable has discussed long term projects to develop a coordinated needs assessment, common acceptance of fiscal and program evaluations, and a comprehensive county-wide human service plan.

The Human Service Coordination Project and the Human Service Funders Roundtable have provided a significant step toward coordination of human service planning and funding, based on the desire to make sense out of confusion and to better utilize scarce resources.

FOOTNOTES

1. This report is available from the Sacramento Regional Area Planning Commission, 800 H Street, Sacramento, California 95804. An up-dated version covering fiscal year 1979 allocations is also available at the same address.

AGENCY COORDINATION: STRUCTURAL AND TECHNICAL APPROACHES

Gilbert Hamilton

The systems concept, widely used in industrial and academic circles, has many interpretations. For the purpose of this paper, a system is defined as a complex set of interacting elements consisting of information, people, and materials. Each part of a system is a subsystem of the whole. The interaction of the elements causes the system to behave as a whole, as changes in any one element result in changes in all others. Competition within the system is universal: the elements within the system and within its parts are always engaged in a competitive struggle.

Systems can be characterized as either closed or open. A closed system behaves differently over time than an open system. In its input-output and feedback requirements, a closed system eventually must reach a state of equilibrium, while an open system reaches a steady state that appears constant but involves a continuous inflow and outflow of information, people, and materials.

Churchman has identified five basic considerations necessary for defining and analyzing systems.[1] He has indicated that any analysis of a system should consider:

1. the total system objectives and, more specifically, the performance of the whole system
2. the system's environment and fixed constraints
3. the resources of the system
4. the components of the system, their activities, goals, and measures of performance, and
5. the management of the system.

To provide an understanding of intra/inter-agency coordination as a function of organizational differentiation and design, this paper will focus on the management of a system.

Within the systems concept, private business organizations and public-supported human service organizations can be viewed as subsystems of a

45

much larger economic system. At the same time, each subsystem can be regarded as a system in itself, with a relationship to the larger whole. Lawrence and Lorsch have further clarified the systems concept and its application to human service organizations.[2] They have contended that the behavior of an organization's members also is related to the formal organization and is influenced by the task to be performed and by the unwritten rules regarding appropriate membership behavior. According to their concept, a person's behavior is determined by his or her needs and motives and by the way his or her personality interacts with the personalities of colleagues and subordinates. Their argument suggests that human relationships within the organization are determined not only by the organization's formal and informal arrangements but also by its rewards, controls, and perceptions regarding the conduct of its members.

The systems approach suggests that the organization interacts with its external environment. As the organization grows larger, it divides into parts, each having the difficult task of coordinating its efforts with a part of the organization's external environment. Since managers have a limited span of surveillance in dealing with the organization's external environment, their capacity to effectively coordinate the organization's efforts with its total environment is restricted. Nevertheless, the parts of the organization must be linked to ensure its survival and the accomplishment of its overall purpose.

Because of differentiation or division of labor, specialization, and attitudinal and behavioral differences among managers in their orientation to the goals of the organization, internal/external coordination is essential if organizational goals and objectives are to be achieved with a maximum of economy and efficiency. The degrees of differentiation and coordination required are determined by the type of organizational structure, the external environment, and the purpose of the organization.

ORGANIZATIONAL DESIGN

Business and human service organizations adopt either a functional or a divisional organizational structure. Each design generates organizational differentiation in agency activities and requires coordination both internally and externally. However, coordination methods used in functional and divisional structures differ significantly in substance and motive.

Functional Structure: The functional structure is regarded as the basic building block of an organization. Perceived by management theorists as the module in which other organizational forms are created, the functional structure is formed after the organization's major work efforts have been clearly identified, defined, and grouped into major departments or units. To simplify coordination within each functional unit, related work is placed in one organizational component under one management head. The functional structure facilitates labor specialization, economy of operation, and economic flexibility. Its pattern of growth encourages the development of a highly centralized vertical hierarchy of skills within the various levels of the organization.

The advantages of the functional structure heavily outweigh the disadvantages. However, as the organization grows and diversifies the disadvantages tend to increase. When the functional structure is highly centralized and specialization is encouraged, there is a tendency toward inflexibility. As growth and diversification foster greater centralization, they often result in excessive delays in managerial decision making, breakdowns in coordination between functions, and difficulties in establishing reasonable and adequate control of workers. When additional organizational levels are added to the functional structure, work slows down because it is more difficult for decisions to filter through to the lower operating levels.

The high degree of centralization in the functional structure encourages a narrow perception of management and its tasks. Each manager is concerned with his or her own specialty and often fails to relate individual performance to the performance of the enterprise as a whole. As the organization grows and diversifies, the degree of organizational differentiation increases since each unit is concerned not with the product itself but with one kind of major work effort going into the product. As a result, the functional unit is insular and inherently difficult to coordinate.[3]

Divisional Structure: Divisional structuring is a means of dividing a large, highly centralized organization into smaller and more flexible administrative units. This type of structure enables the organization to recapture many of the advantages of a small functional organization, while minimizing the disadvantages that come with increasing size and diversity. The divisional structure is formed through the creation of a number of smaller autonomous units within the organization. These units may be organized according to product, programs, or geography. In the case of product or programs, divisionalization focuses the major effort of the organization on the needs of the markets being served and their constituents.

The development process of the divisional structure often involves the dismemberment of an existing highly centralized functional structure. The move toward divisionalization therefore can be expensive and wasteful of both manpower and facilities. Since in the divisionalized organization managerial concern is primarily with the operating objectives of each autonomous unit, effective coordination of units is difficult to achieve. Managers of each division must rely on organizational objectives and policies and on a specialized central staff to facilitate coordination. In contrast to the central authority exercised in the functional structure, coordinating capability is usually built into the divisional structure. Once established, coordination is usually easier to maintain in a divisional structure than in a functional one, as the point of coordination reaches lower into the organizational structure and tends to bring the functional heads into closer contact.

A cursory review of the two types of organizational structure indicates that both are highly differentiated and that the orientation of staff members to organizational goals and objectives can differ significantly from one type to the other. In the functional structure, the work of the organization is identified and defined by the administrative head, who subsequently delegates the work to the appropriate functional units. Over time, the units become highly specialized and each assumes a subgroup identity with its own set of values, goals, and objectives. When this differentiation occurs, integrative conflict emerges among units at lower levels. This conflict must be reconciled by the administrative head, who serves as the coordinating authority in organizing the work effort.

Since in the functional structure one administrative head organizes the work, the authority and responsibility of the organization's members must depend on their positions within the structure. This conclusion is based on the assumption that the knowledge of an individual occupying a specific position is commensurate with his organizational influence and leadership. In the functional structure, few opportunities exist for subordinate participation in organizational decision making. The administrative head has the responsibility not only of internal coordination but also of coordination of the efforts of the organization with its external environment.

In the divisional structure, while management is concerned primarily with the operating objectives of each autonomous unit, the specialized central coordinating staff integrates the activities of each division. The members of the coordinating staff are highly placed in the organization and have the capability to act with authority, although this capability is not always demonstrated. Recruited on the basis of their extensive knowledge of organizational activities and their tenure, they generally command the respect of all organizational members. When there is a breakdown in coordination between divisions, these individuals intervene to resolve the conflict, with the interest of the organization in mind.

As has been shown, a business or human service organization may adopt a functional or a divisional organizational structure, the choice being determined mainly by the organization's size and scope of operation. When a business is under single ownership or limited partnership and is small in terms of both product line and number of employees, a functional structure is generally more desirable. This type of structure centralizes all organizational decisions under one administrative body and enhances organizational survival in a competitive environment through labor specialization, economy of operation, and economic flexibility. The functional structure has similar advantages for small, single program/project human service organizations.

However, as each organization grows and diversifies, in terms of product line and market for business organizations and programs/projects for human service organizations, the divisional structure becomes more necessary to the achievement of coordination. As either a business or a human service organization grows — often for reasons of survival — its operation becomes more complex and difficult to manage. This management is particularly difficult if the growth is unplanned, since errors in resource allocation, manpower utilization, and service and task duplication result in an inefficient and ineffective organization.

Business organizations have been more aware than human service organizations of the high dollar-cost associated with inadequate coordination. The needs of business organizations to maximize profits and to increase market share in providing goods and services in order to survive have made this awareness essential. To achieve these objectives, business organizations must constantly be aware of the cost factors involved in conducting business; they have therefore devised several techniques to ensure economy of operation through coordination. Using the systems concept, they have developed two techniques for management planning, scheduling, and control which can be integrated into the organization's internal and external environment to achieve coordination of organizational activities. These techniques, called the Program/Project Evaluation and Review Technique (PERT) and the Critical Path Method (CPM), involve the development of program/project networks that interphase functional and divisional boundaries and the organization's external environment, including consumers, governmental agencies, legislative bodies, and competitors. These program/project network techniques identify and define the work to be performed, who will perform it, where it will be performed, when it will be performed, and the interdependent relationship of the work and the organizational objectives.

By using the network approach, business organizations avoid the problems and the dollar-cost of inadequate coordination. Business organizations have used this approach regardless of the type of enterprise or product mix and in either functional structures (where the administrative head is responsible for agency coordination) or divisional structures (where a central specialized coordinating staff is utilized). The success of the widespread use of PERT and CPM in business organizations indicates that these techniques could be equally successful in human service organizations, since business and human service managers have the same responsibility: to achieve organizational goals and objectives through others.

HUMAN SERVICE ORGANIZATIONS

Human service organizations and their managers have been reluctant to accept PERT and/or CPM as management techniques. They have relied instead, with varying success, on the traditional coordination elements inherent in the functional and divisional structures. One reason given for the lack of acceptance of PERT and/or CPM is that managers have limited technical knowledge of them and little exposure to the usefulness of these techniques in management. This position is supported by a recent human service management survey conducted by the Institute for Human Service Management.[4] This survey of approximately three hundred managers, or management types, in a large state social service agency revealed that they had little knowledge of the use of PERT and/or CPM as management techniques.

A second reason for not accepting these techniques is advanced by supporters of the human service delivery system who claim that human service organizations are different from business organizations and that the management tools and techniques developed in and for business usually are not appropriate for human service organizations. These individuals argue that human service organizations differ from other bureaucracies in that they are usually tax-supported organizations designed to maintain and improve the well-being and functioning of people through the delivery of services. Their input is people with specific attributes; their output is people processed or changed in a predetermined manner.[5] While business organizations deal with inanimate raw materials, human service organizations deal with human beings, who can assess the worth of a service delivered and its impact upon their condition. While the goals of business organizations are specific and easily measurable, the goals of human service organizations express primarily ideological commitments, which are intangible and difficult to measure.

However, it appears that traditional approaches to coordination in human service organizations will no longer suffice. Citing such deficiencies as discrepancy between organizational objectives and performance, insensitive service mechanisms, and wasteful and inefficient management practices, critics suggest that human service organizations should become more businesslike.[6] Californians have recently acted on their concerns by passing a tax-limitation measure restricting the resource base of tax-supported organizations.[7]

As public expenditure in support of their efforts decreases and competition within the system for limited resources intensifies, human service organizations find themselves confronted with complex service delivery and organizational crises. These organizations must undertake service and organizational analyses to assist them in using their existing resources more efficiently and effectively by coordinating their internal activities with their external environment. Since an organization's ability to plan, schedule, and control its activities is vital to coordination, it is suggested that human service organizations can and should incorporate management techniques such as PERT and CPM which are employed successfully in the business sector.

PROGRAM/PROJECT EVALUATION AND REVIEW TECHNIQUE AND CRITICAL PATH METHOD

In the United States in 1957 and 1958, two management planning, scheduling, and control techniques were developed which have utility for facilitating inter/intra-organizational coordination. The first was the Program/Project Evaluation and Review Technique (PERT), developed by the Lockheed Corporation,[8] and the second was the Critical Path Method (CPM), developed by the Sperry Rand Corporation.[9]

During their developmental stages, each technique was perceived as distinct from the other. However, frequent use has caused the difference between the two to become less pronounced. Each can be used to coordinate and schedule activities in varying work situations and neither is directly suitable to repetitive task operations. Both are based on a network concept and identify critical paths and float or slack time within the network. Since the concepts are virtually the same in each technique, this discussion will focus on PERT as an integrative approach to the two. The basic concepts of PERT and its utility in the planning, scheduling, and control process are discussed here.

PERT CONCEPTS

The basic units in the PERT analysis are the individual jobs (activities) in each major work assignment that are designed to achieve an intended project outcome. Individual jobs which are time or resource consuming are represented by arrows (see Figure 1).

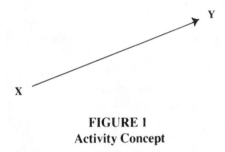

FIGURE 1
Activity Concept

The tail of the arrow (X) represents the start of the job, the shaft of the arrow the progress in the job, and the head of the arrow (Y) the end of the job.

The event or node is the point at which one or more activities terminate and/or one or more activities start. The events have no time duration; they indicate only the transition point between activities. Each event can have one or more activities leading in or out. The two concepts — activities and events or nodes — combine to form the logic of the network (see Figure 2).

In Figure 2a, event or node 1 represents the transition point between the two activities A and B. It cannot occur before activity A is completed, because the arrow representing activity A leads into event 1. Similarly, activity B cannot occur until activity A has been completed, because B leads out of event 1. In Figure 2b, activity E depends on activities C and D; hence, activity E cannot start until activities C and D are completed. Figure 2c represents the situation in which activities G and H depend on the completion of activity F; when activity F is complete, activities G and H are free to start. In network analysis, no event is considered accomplished until all

52

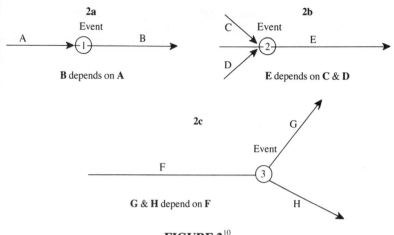

FIGURE 2[10]
Network Elements

work represented by the arrows leading to it has been completed. Additionally, until an event is completed no work can begin on a succeeding activity.

PERT PLANNING PROCESS

The PERT planning phase combines the activity and event concepts and forms a network consisting of all the individual jobs in a project and their relationships to each other. However, prior to network development, the PERT project planning phase should contain the seven elements in Figure 3.

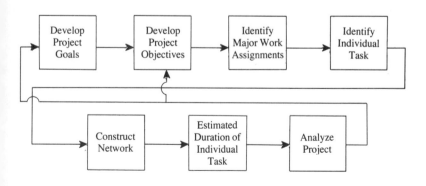

FIGURE 3
Project Planning Elements

The planning elements in the top row in Figure 3 are self-explanatory. Network construction (after each individual job is identified), appropriate time estimates, and project analysis are presented in Figure 4.

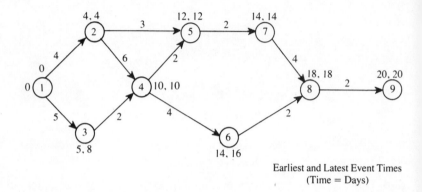

Earliest and Latest Event Times
(Time = Days)

FIGURE 4[11]
PERT Network and Analysis

In viewing Figure 4, it should be assumed that an organizational project has been selected, individual tasks identified, and a network developed and agreed upon by all individuals who are going to perform the activities.

In PERT, the time required to complete each activity is derived from three estimates representing the project team's best knowledge of the time required to achieve the objective and event. Together, the three time estimates, called optimistic, most likely, and pessimistic, represent a realistic activity duration because they deal with likelihood rather than certainty. The estimated time, called the expected time (te), of each activity in Figure 4 is determined from the three time estimates and the beta distribution,[12] for example:

$$te = \frac{a + 4m + b}{6}$$

a = Optimistic time
m = Most likely time
b = Pessimistic time

54

The first step in the PERT analysis is to determine the earliest expected time (TE) that each event will occur, assuming that all previous activities have been accomplished within the time anticipated. The earliest expected time for each event is the sum of the expected times (te) for all preceding activities within a single path from start to finish. Thus, the project network in Figure 4 starts at zero time. Since activity (1, 2) is a 4-day job, the earliest expected completion time of event 2 is 4 days. Similarly, the earliest expected time of completion of event 3 is 5 days.

Event 4 represents a situation where more than one activity leads into an event. When this occurs, the earliest expected time is the greatest sum of the activities leading into the event within a single path. Thus, activity (1, 3) takes 5 days and activity (3, 4) takes 2 days, totalling 7 days; however, activity (1, 2) takes 4 days and activity (2, 4) takes 6 days, totalling 10 days. Therefore, the earliest expected time for event 4 is 10 days. Similarly, the earliest expected time for event 5 is 12 days. Events 6 and 7 take 14 days each, while the earliest expected time for event 8, with two activities leading into it, is 18 days. Assuming that all activities are completed within the time anticipated, the earliest expected time (TE) of completion of the total project is 20 days.

The second step in the analysis in Figure 4 is to determine the latest expected time (TL) in which each event will be completed if the project is to be completed within the time allocated. The latest event time is determined by starting from the total time allocated and working backward from finish to start, subtracting the preceding activity time from the earliest expected time of the event. Since the scheduled completion time of the project is 20 days, the latest expected time of completion of event 8 is 18 days. The latest time for event 7 is 14 days; event 6 is 16 days; event 5 is 12 days; and event 4 is 10 days. Whenever there is more than one activity starting from an event, offering a choice of latest time, the smallest difference is selected as the latest time for the event; thus, event 2 has a latest completion of 4 days. Event 3 has 8 days and event 1, the starting event, has no time duration.

The third step in the analysis is to determine the slack or float time and critical path between events in the network. Some events may be completed later than the earliest expected time without detrimental effects on the achievement of the project's scheduled objectives. However, managers must have knowledge of the slack time and the critical path, since they affect the balance and time trade-offs that might be made between high slack and low slack areas.

The critical path is the series of activities in the network that must start and finish on time if the total project is to be completed within the time allocated. The difference between the earliest expected completion time and latest expected completion time is zero. In order to identify the critical path in the network, the slack time must first be determined by subtracting the earliest expected time from the latest expected time (TL-TE) for each event (see Figure 5). The slack time indicates the number of days, weeks, months, etc. remaining if the event is to be completed by the earliest expected event time. If the difference TL-TE is zero, there is no slack time and the activity leading into the event is in the critical path.

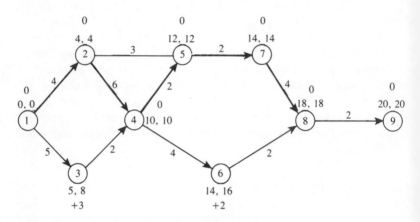

FIGURE 5
Slack Time Analysis

The critical path in Figure 5 is represented by the darker arrow. Since a critical path has zero slack time in the network, it contains events that can become troublesome to managers if each activity in the path is not balanced and timed on schedule. These are the areas in which slippage can occur, hindering the organization's ability to coordinate the project within the allotted time frame. However, by locating the events having significant slack time, managers can exercise some flexibility in effecting trade-offs in resources and personnel with those events having little or no slack time. As an example, event 3 in Figure 5 has 3 days' slack time and event 6 has 2 days'. These events could be delayed 2 to 3 days without causing slippage in the overall program schedule. The slack time and critical path identified in the network allow management to utilize manpower and balance activities more effectively and efficiently. The PERT analysis can be summarized as in Figure 6.

Event	Preceding Event(s)	te	TE	TL	TL-TE
9	8	2	20	20	0.0
8	7	4	18	18	0.0
	6	2	18	18	0.0
7	5	2	14	14	0.0
6	4	4	14	16	2.0
5	4	2	12	12	0.0
	2	3	12	12	0.0
4	2	6	10	10	0.0
	3	2	10	10	0.0
3	1	5	5	8	3.0
2	1	4	4	4	0.0

FIGURE 6
PERT Analysis

CONCLUSION

The PERT approach to achieving balanced, phased timing, and service integration emphasizes the interdependencies of agency operations in both functional and divisional organizational structures. The network concept links together spatially the various elements of the human service delivery system. The network design forming the human service delivery system can be represented in a hierarchical arrangement of local, state, and federal jurisdictions, each level within the hierarchy functioning as a subsystem of the whole.

The network design and its activities are derived from the objectives of each level within the organization. The work activity of each level forms the input to the work activities of succeeding levels. In the hierarchical network schema, the constraints imposed on lower level human service subsystems are a function of the goal orientations of higher order subsystems and of the environment of the system as a whole. Because of relationships, the lack of an organized management technique can cause the system to be wasteful and ineffective in the pursuit of its goals and objectives. The adoption of PERT on a system-wide basis as an organized management technique can enhance the ability to coordinate and integrate projects, programs, and planned activities within and among human service organizations.

However, the application of PERT cannot be viewed as the solution to all problems of coordination in human service organizations. Some of these problems can be solved through the organizational structure and through the personal leadership of the organizational head or coordinating staff. Others can be solved through the willingness of competing human service organizations to share or consolidate their activities to enhance their ability to survive. Nevertheless, PERT does offer a management approach that clarifies the goals and objectives of an organization and structures its work effort for the improvement of effectiveness and efficiency through coordination.

FOOTNOTES

1. West Churchman, *The Systems Approach* (New York: Delacourt Press, 1968).

2. Paul Lawrence and Jay Lorsch, *Organization and Environment, Managing Differentiation and Integration* (Cambridge, Mass.: Harvard University Press, 1967).

3. Louis A. Allen, *Management and Organizations* (New York: McGraw-Hill Series in Management, 1958).

4. For complete information, contact the Institute for Human Service Management, 1401 21st Street, Sacramento, California 95814.

5. Yeheskel Hasenfeld and Richard A. English, *Human Service Organizations* (Ann Arbor: The University of Michigan Press, 1974), p. 1.

6. Ibid., p. 3.

7. State of California Tax Initiative, Proposition 13, limiting the assessed valuation of privately owned real estate, improved and unimproved.

8. PERT was developed by C. E. Clark, W. Eagen, D. G. Malcolm, and J.H. Roseboom working with the management consulting firm of Booze, Allen and Hamilton, the Navy Bureau of Ordinance, and Lockheed Corporation.

9. The basic development is attributable to M. R. Walker who was with the Engineering Service Division of E. I. De Nemours & Company, Inc., and J. E. Kelley, Jr., Remington Rand Univac (now Sperry Rand Corporation).

10. Paul Barnetson, *Critical Path Planning: Present and Future Techniques* (London: Newnes-Butterworths, 1969).

11. Ibid.

12. David I. Cleland and William R. King, *Systems, Organizations Analysis, Management: A Book of Readings* (New York: McGraw-Hill Book Company, 1969).

REFERENCES

Allen, Louis A. *Management and Organizations*. New York: McGraw-Hill Series in Management, 1958.

Barnetson, Paul. *Critical Path Planning: Present and Future Techniques*. London: Newnes-Butterworths, 1969.

Churchman, West. *The Systems Approach*. New York: Delacourt Press, 1968.

Cleland, David I. and King, William R. *Systems, Organizations Analysis, Management: A Book of Readings*. New York: McGraw-Hill Book Company, 1969.

Hasenfeld, Yeheskel and English, Richard A. *Human Service Organizations*. Ann Arbor: University of Michigan Press, 1974.

PART 2

ACHIEVING HUMAN SERVICE GOALS

The authors in this section of the book focus on the utilization of resources to achieve organizational goals. Their papers look at three types of resources used in achieving human service results: people, methods, and finances.

PEOPLE

Four of the papers in this section focus directly on realizing the potential of people in a human service organization. While they look at this issue from diverse perspectives, these authors all stress the need to facilitate effective linkages between individual and organizational goals.

Using a behavioral perspective, Anton looks at concrete ways of individualizing organizational approaches to personnel. He suggests that the behavioral approach moves away from a haphazard manner of dealing with people and provides a more systematic method of improving performance by increasing job satisfaction.

Van Luijtelaar and Pecenka consider the relationship of employee development to organizational development. Contrary to the traditional view in American literature, organizational development is most effective when it ensures the participation of employees from all levels of the organization rather than merely those at the top. These authors offer a unique approach to facilitating the development of people throughout an organization.

Gill looks at some ways of improving the functioning of task force groups. In her view, leadership is critical to accomplishment but cannot be effective without an operational understanding of individual and group dynamics. This concern is especially important given the tendency of organizations to create *ad hoc* groups to cope with emerging issues and problems.

Ferman's paper looks at bargaining, one of the latest developments in human service management. Though the issues are similar to those in other sectors, the human service organization again provides some unique twists in the bargaining process. In a detailed discussion, Ferman outlines the major steps to achieving a working agreement.

METHODS

Four papers in this section look at methods which can be used to promote greater coordination of resources in an organization. Shiffler looks at Management By Objectives (MBO) as a means of improving operating results. In this analysis he provides some much needed comparisons and contrasts between the business organization and the human service organization in the implementation of an MBO program.

Babcock and Sorensen look at the need for compatibility between management systems and the methods used by organizations to produce their products. The authors' analysis of two different human service organizations is based on the idea that the effectiveness of participative and nonparticipative management is mediated by the type of treatment technology utilized by the organization. They believe that the matching of organizational management with technology holds promise for improving the effectiveness of human service organizations.

Holland's paper views information as a major resource in the human service organization. Systematic methods of collecting, processing, and utilizing information are rare in most areas of the human services. Holland presents the issues to be considered in developing effective information systems and points to the need for developing them in a way compatible with the goals of the organization.

Ford discusses the role of the manager as an exchange agent between the organization and the many components of its task environment. To function effectively in this role, the manager must know how to transmit to decision makers within the organization information about the forces for change in the environment and how to interpret the organization's goals to its constituents. In Ford's view, the importance of the boundary-spanning activities of the manager is growing with the increasing influence of the environment on organizations.

FINANCES

The last two papers in this section take very different approaches to providing insight into financial management for human service organizations. Thompson, on the one hand, looks at potential ways of utilizing finances at the macro level to achieve more effective performance in human service organizations.

Lazarus, on the other hand, looks at some of the "nuts and bolts" of budgeting for the small- to intermediate-sized human service agency. His description of the steps involved in budget development and implementation emphasizes the importance of budgeting in providing information for evaluation.

JOB SATISFACTION:
A BEHAVIORAL APPROACH

Paul Anton

What is job satisfaction? In attempting to answer this provocative question, Locke has observed that, although probably more than four thousand articles were published on the subject between 1930 and 1969, "... our understanding of the *causes* of job satisfaction has not advanced at a pace commensurate with research results."[1]

Many academics and practitioners have blamed operationalism "... for the frequent failure of psychologists to understand the processes they are measuring."[2] Although they are especially disdainful of Skinner's "descriptive behaviorism [for treating] men and animals as empty organisms,"[3] they not infrequently observe that "... there is still confusion over whether the determinants [of job satisfaction] lie solely in the job itself (the intrinsic view), whether they reside wholly in the worker's mind (the subjective view), or whether satisfaction is the consequence of an interaction between the worker and his environment."[4]

Commenting on this dilemma, Skinner has stated that:

Feelings and states of mind still dominate discussions of human behavior for many reasons. For one thing, they have long obscured the alternatives that might replace them; it is hard to see behavior as such without reading into it many of the things it is said to express . . . . Until contingencies [of reinforcement] had been arranged and their effects studied in the laboratory, little effort was made to find them in daily life.[5]

Thus, it would seem that to pursue an understanding of the causes of job satisfaction by interpreting the unspecified aspects of human behavior will neither eliminate the confusion nor ensure the achievement of job satisfaction. It seems reasonable, therefore, to consider other paths to an understanding of job satisfaction.

To enhance its goal-seeking activities, an organization usually strives for certainty, uniformity, standardization, and minimal risk. While perhaps necessary and important for the organization, these constraints may be incompatible with an individual's own expectations, demonstrated diversity, and concern with job satisfaction and/or self-fulfillment. A common prescription for the ills that plague organizations is a universal organizational and/or motivational design that proposes to cope with the nagging problems of individual differences.

Organizations and their managers need a mechanism for accommodating these individual difference variables on a systematic basis and relating them to organizational goals. To use such a mechanism, organizations must be individualized rather than homogenized. If we assume that the goal in the individual/organizational interface is greater job satisfaction for the former and greater efficiency and productivity (i.e., profitability) for the latter, it may be useful to examine the potential of an operationally driven model to explain job satisfaction.

THE INDIVIDUAL/ORGANIZATIONAL INTERFACE

One exceedingly important yet very perplexing aspect of human behavior is seen when evaluations or judgments are made of the performance of an individual at any level by the organization(s) with which he or she is involved. Most commonly, the organization measures the individual's output in relation to some standard (e.g., production, grade point, profits, income, quotas, etc.). If the job is done as well as or better than the standard (usually established unilaterally by the organization), then management is presumed to have been effective. If job performance is not up to the standard, it is assumed that the individual is at fault and he or she is expected to adjust.

Organizational expectations of people's motivations are derived from the assumptions of some theorists that although people may differ in potential they are basically homogeneous in needs and behavior patterns.[6] These expectations have led to fruitless and costly efforts by managers to find an organizational design which would guarantee success in handling people. Lawler has noted that, in spite of these efforts,

> . . . validity coefficients have seldom exceeded .50. One reason for this seems to be that they [the organizational psychologists] have never developed good predictive measures of a person's motivation to do the job. In short, they can predict fairly well whether the person can do the job but not at all whether he will do it.[7]

There is increasing evidence too that people's responses to many of the organization's expectations of their motivations (e.g., money, status, responsibility, job enrichment) are far from uniform.[8] The demonstrated difficulty in predicting human behavior in general is proof of human variety. Growing worker alienation, declining productivity, reluctance to work for overtime pay and other standard incentives, and demands for more recognition, more leisure, early retirement, and so on, bear witness to the problem.

As organizations continue to expand and change, the diversity of the work force will increase, further emphasizing individual differences. As Lawler has suggested, this development would seem to require that an organization begin ". . . measuring individual difference variables for the purpose of placing people in jobs and as an aid in designing job situations to fit people."[9] Thus, there may be a need to move away from the search for the "best way" to treat people and design organizations, and to seek instead, as suggested, a means of accommodating these real individual difference variables in a systematic way.

A possible approach to this problem is to view an organization (and its people) behaviorally and operationally as a series of relative reinforcement events. The logic for this approach is developed from the positive reinforcement analyses made by Premack, Bansal, Brownstein, Foley, Schaeffer *et al.,* and others, which lead to a relative reflex strength definition of reinforcement.[10] The implications of these analyses may provide a basis for redefining individual performance in terms of specific discriminable behaviors.

A description of relative reinforcement specifies that given any two responses having different independent rates of occurrence in a contingent response situation, the higher rate response will reinforce (i.e., increase the rate of) the lower rate response but not vice versa. Thus, any stimulus to which a response can be observed can act as a reinforcer, provided only that its probability of occurrence is greater than that of some other response.

This view is supported by the experience of Charlesworth, who was faced with the need for changing the so-called poverty syndrome among people in Appalachian Kentucky (". . . the conviction held by many people that they have no control over their own destiny [as] evidenced among many inhabitants by a fatalistic indifference toward the future").[11] His success in changing this pervasive attitude was achieved behaviorally through the introduction of a change agent.

> *Basically, what the change agent approach does is to implement a behavioral model of man. Such a model claims that the great majority of behavior patterns are established and maintained by what is described as differential reinforcement of human activities — such reinforcements taking place after an activity has occurred . . . . Not all behavioral patterns are encouraged. Only those deemed desirable by a group or society are rewarded, others are not, and still others may be punished. [12]*

Convinced of the efficacy of applying Skinnerian operant principles to the solution of managerial problems, Nord has described the experience of a leading St. Louis, Missouri, hardware company in applying an approximate variable ratio schedule of reinforcement to help solve a substantial problem of absenteeism and tardiness. Using a lottery system, employees who were on time (not so much as half a minute late) for a month were eligible for a drawing of prizes valued from $20 to $25. At the end of each six-month period, persons without absences were eligible for a drawing for a color television. When reported by Nord, the program had been in operation for sixteen months and, according to the firm's personnel director, had reduced sick leave costs by about sixty-two percent. Conditions which had been a very serious problem ". . . have greatly improved." Observed Nord, "The possibilities [of using differential reinforcement techniques] for other areas are limited largely by the creativity of management." [13]

Premack has provided evidence that reinforcement is not only predictable but also reversible. He demonstrated that in rats drinking could be made more probable than running, or vice versa, simply by altering the parameters in determining which response would likely have the higher rate. In each case, the more probable response, as independently determined, reinforced the less probable one. [14]

These events contradict traditional reinforcement theory, which tends to assign reinforcement capabilities to certain behaviors and not to others. Meehl has written that reinforcement is transsituational (i.e., a reinforcer in one situation is a reinforcer in all situations). [15] This theory suggests that reinforcement effects and relationships are fixed and predetermined. Premack has commented on the fundamental differences between relative reinforcement and the traditional concepts:

> *The traditional vocabulary of drive, reward, and goal becomes either meaningless or misleading, for [my] model leads to the prediction that (i) the eating or drinking response is itself reinforc-*

ible and, more important, (ii) the reinforcement relation is reversible. This relationship suggests that a "reward" is simply any response that is independently more probable than another response. [16]

It appears that relative reinforcement effects or outcomes can be termed response-defined events. There may be a synergy between them that can aid managers to individualize their organizations. Since they address the problems of capitalizing on individual difference variables, these differences must be identified.

By utilizing the behavioral aspects of reinforcement which have been discussed here, attention can be directed to those phenomena that are observable and thus measurable. This approach does not deny the existence of complex response mechanisms within the individual, but rather emphasizes that the source of most of our basic data about man has been his more easily observable behavior. As Premack has indicated, "Anatomically different responses can be compared directly . . . [and] an indifference principle holds such that the reinforcement value is determined by response probability independent of parameters used to produce the probability or kind of response that manifests the probability." [17]

Thus, an explicit, discrete, verbal and/or nonverbal communicational-psychological job profile instrument can be developed based on the response patterns required (in terms of the needs of the organization) to do a specified job. A related analysis can be made for individuals to determine in advance what the probability is of their responding in certain ways to the specified job stimuli. Appropriate means have been developed to ascertain these independent probabilities.

These profiles of job and individual are then scanned (simply and quickly by machine) for any positive contingent reinforcement potential. If the probable response patterns of job and individual are compatible, parameters can be devised for necessary contingent reinforcement effects which should increase the level of performance. It has been established empirically that contingent higher rate independent responses will reinforce (increase the rate of) preceding lower rate responses *without regard to the structural characteristics of the responses involved,* the only stipulations being that the responses must not compete and that the rate differential must be independently determined.

A procedure such as that outlined here is designed to simplify and significantly improve the organizational processes of personnel development by allowing both the organization and the individual to make job decisions based on observable and measurable responses to specific stimuli. Indeed, if the conditions are met, the individual's own reinforcement behavior patterns will be utilized to maximize his or her productivity. Much of what now occurs is based on chance, at great cost to the individual, the organization, and the community.

The suggested procedure provides also a potential for integrating into the work force large numbers of people who are now classified as unemployable because their abilities cannot be measured by traditional instruments requiring standardized language or other skills. Without specialized training, education, or even a common language, but using simply his ability to respond in predetermined ways to specified stimuli, an individual can match his performance potential with the requirements of an appropriate job.

Without such a mechanism, the problem of determining what is meaningful for people in an organization becomes overwhelming. As Weisman has noted:

> . . . *the word,* meaning, *represents a great range of diverse matters, such as: denotation; connotation; neuro-muscular and glandular activity; usefulness; value; conceptual implications; to what the interpreter of a symbol refers; to what the interpreter of a symbol ought to be referring; what the user of a symbol wants the interpreter to infer; or for that matter, any object of consciousness whatsoever.*[18]

Measures have been suggested here for enlarging organizations by "individualizing" them using a systematic, behavioral, operationally determined relationship. This approach eliminates some of the confusing demands made on people by standardization, specialization, and simplification, which have perpetuated the notion that industrialization leads to dehumanization. By increasing productivity and decreasing problems, the application of the principles discussed in this paper may have positive consequences for both individuals and organizations. However,

> . . . *more of this type of research is needed if individualized organizations are to build on the basis of research knowledge rather than intuition.*
>
> *There simply is little information with respect to how different individuals react to such job characteristics as uncertainty and*

communication load and how different individuals should be communicated with. In many cases, it is not even known what the relevant individual difference variables are, when consideration is being given to predicting how people will react to different administrative procedures, policies, or to different organizational climates.[19]

FOOTNOTES

1. E. A. Locke, "What is Job Satisfaction?" *Organizational Behavior and Human Performance* 4 (1969): 309.

2. Ibid., p. 313.

3. Ibid., p. 311.

4. Ibid., p. 309.

5. B. F. Skinner, *Beyond Freedom and Dignity* (New York: Knopf, 1971), p. 147.

6. For instance, A. H. Maslow, "A Theory of Human Motivation," *Psychological Review* 50 (Jan.-Nov. 1943): 370-96; E. Mayo, *The Social Problems of an Industrial Civilization* (Cambridge, Mass.: Harvard University Press, 1945); D. McClelland, *The Achieving Society* (Princeton, N.J.: D. Van Nostrand Co., 1961); D. McGregor, *The Human Side of Enterprise* (New York: McGraw-Hill, 1960); F. J. Roethlisberger and W. J. Dickson, *Management and the Worker* (Cambridge, Mass.: Harvard University Press, 1939); and F. W. Taylor, *Principles of Scientific Management* (New York: Harpers, 1911).

7. E. E. Lawler III, "Individualizing Organizations," paper presented at Midwestern Psychological Association Convention, Chicago, May 1970, p. 2.

8. E. Berne, *The Structure and Dynamics of Organizations and Groups* (New York: Grove Press, 1963); S. Demczynski, *Automation and the Future of Man* (London: George Allen and Unwin, Ltd., 1964); W. W.

Porter and E. E. Lawler III, *Managerial Attitudes and Performance* (Homewood, Ill.: Richard D. Irwin, 1968); and W. A. Weisskopf, *Alienation and Economics* (New York: E. P. Dutton, 1971).

9. Lawler, 1970, p. 15.

10. A. K. Bansal, "Relative Reinforcement Effectiveness of Referential and Non-Referential Word Structures" (Master's thesis, Ohio University, 1970); A. J. Brownstein, "Predicting Instrumental Performance from the Independent Rates of Contingent Responses in a Choice Situation," *Journal of Experimental Psychology* 63 (Jan. 1962): 29-31; A. J. Foley, "Reflex Complexity as a Factor of Reinforcement Effectiveness in a Relative Reflex Strength Situation" (Master's thesis, Ohio University, 1968); R. W. Schaeffer *et al.*, "Positive Reinforcement: A Test of the Premack Theory," *Psychonomic Science* 4 (Jan. 5, 1966): 7-8; and D. Premack, "Rate Differential Reinforcement in Monkey Manipulation," *Journal of Experimental Analysis of Behavior* 6 (Jan. 1963): 81-89.

11. H. K. Charlesworth, *Small Scale Entrepreneurs: The Forgotten Men in Economic Planning and Development* (Lexington, Kentucky: Office of Business Development and Government Services, College of Business and Economics, University of Kentucky, May 29, 1973), p. 6.

12. Ibid., p. 8.

13. W. R. Nord, "Beyond the Teaching Machine: The Neglected Area of Operant Conditioning in the Theory and Practice of Management," *Organizational Behavior and Human Performance* 4 (1969): 375-401.

14. D. Premack, "Toward Empirical Behavior Laws," *Psychological Review* 66 (July 1959): 219-33.

15. R. E. Meehl, "On the Circularity of the Law of Effect," *Psychological Bulletin* 47 (Jan. 1950): 52-75.

16. D. Premack, "Reversibility of the Reinforcement Relation," *Science* 136 (Jan.-June 1962): 255.

17. D. Premack, "Reinforcement Theory," in *Nebraska Symposium on Motivation,* ed. D. Levine (Lincoln: University of Nebraska Press, 1965), p. 132.

18. H. M. Weisman, "Problems in Meaning," in *Managerial Control Through Communication,* eds. G. T. Vardaman and C. C. Halterman (New York: John Wiley, 1968), p. 193.

19. Lawler, 1970, p. 10.

REFERENCES

Bansal, A. K. "Relative Reinforcement Effectiveness of Referential and Non-Referential Word Structures." Master's thesis, Ohio University, 1970.

Berne, E. *The Structure and Dynamics of Organizations and Groups.* New York: Grove Press, 1963.

Brownstein, A. J. "Predicting Instrumental Performance from the Independent Rates of Contingent Responses in a Choice Situation." *Journal of Experimental Psychology* 63 (Jan. 1962): 29-31.

Charlesworth, H. K. *Small Scale Entrepreneurs: The Forgotten Men in Economic Planning and Development.* Lexington, Kentucky: Office of Business Development and Government Services, College of Business and Economics, University of Kentucky, May 29, 1973.

Demczynski, S. *Automation and the Future of Man.* London: George Allen and Unwin, Ltd., 1964.

Foley, A. J. "Reflex Complexity as a Factor of Reinforcement Effectiveness in a Relative Reflex Strength Situation." Master's thesis, Ohio University, 1968.

Lawler, E. E. III. "Individualizing Organizations." Paper presented at Midwestern Psychological Association Convention, Chicago, May 1970.

Locke, E. A. "What is Job Satisfaction?" *Organizational Behavior and Human Performance* 4 (1969): 309.

Maslow, A. H. "A Theory of Human Motivation." *Psychological Review* 50 (Jan.-Nov. 1943): 370-96.

Mayo, E. *The Social Problems of an Industrial Civilization.* Cambridge, Mass.: Harvard University Press, 1945.

McClelland, D. *The Achieving Society.* Princeton, N.J.: D. Van Nostrand Co., 1961.

McGregor, D. *The Human Side of Enterprise.* New York: McGraw-Hill, 1960.

Meehl, R. E. "On the Circularity of the Law of Effect." *Psychological Bulletin* 47 (Jan. 1950): 52-75.

Nord, W. R. "Beyond the Teaching Machine: The Neglected Area of

Operant Conditioning in the Theory and Practice of Management." *Organizational Behavior and Human Performance* 4 (1969): 375-401.

Porter, W. W., and Lawler, E.E. III. *Managerial Attitudes and Performance*. Homewood, Ill.: Richard D. Irwin, 1968.

Premack, D. "Toward Empirical Behavior Laws." *Psychological Review* 66 (July 1959): 219-33.

Premack, D. "Predicting Instrumental Performance from the Independent Rate of the Contingent Response." *Journal of Experimental Psychology* 61 (Jan. 1961): 163-71.

Premack, D. "Reversibility of the Reinforcement Relation." *Science* 136 (Jan.-June 1962): 255-57.

Premack, D. "Rate Differential Reinforcement in Monkey Manipulation." *Journal of Experimental Analysis of Behavior* 6 (Jan. 1963): 81-89.

Premack, D. "Reinforcement Theory." In *Nebraska Symposium on Motivation,* pp. 123-88. Edited by D. Levine. Lincoln: University of Nebraska Press, 1965.

Roethlisberger, F. J., and Dickson, W. J. *Management and the Worker*. Cambridge, Mass.: Harvard University Press, 1939.

Schaeffer, R. W.; Hanna, B.; and Russo, P. "Positive Reinforcement: A Test of the Premack Theory." *Psychonomic Science* 4 (Jan. 5, 1966): 7-8.

Skinner, B. F. *Beyond Freedom and Dignity*. New York: Knopf, 1971.

Taylor, F. W. *Principles of Scientific Management*. New York: Harpers, 1911.

Weisman, H. M. "Problems in Meaning." In *Managerial Control Through Communication,* p. 193. Edited by G. T. Vardaman and C. C. Halterman. New York: John Wiley, 1968.

Weisskopf, W. A. *Alienation and Economics*. New York: E. P. Dutton, 1971.

ORGANIZATION DEVELOPMENT AND EMPLOYEE PARTICIPATION

Toine van Luijtelaar
Joseph O. Pecenka

Organization development (OD) is an evolving field, with an objective of enhancing organizational effectiveness and efficiency. Management development (MD) programs of an earlier era concentrated on the development of skills to improve managers' performance on the job and/or to fit them for promotion. In the mid-1940s, many management experts began to suggest that there were better ways to optimize successful performance and decision making in organizations. They suggested that the first step was to change the interactional attitudes and habits of organizational members, fostering in them a frame of mind to achieve organizational potentials for solving problems, confronting conflicts, formulating policies, and handling operational matters more effectively.

Later views have included the changing of functional processes,[1] OD currently is seen as a continuing effort by organizations, typically with the help of outside consultants, "to uncover and remove attitudinal, behavioral, procedural, policy, and structural barriers to effective performance across the entire sociotechnical system, gaining in the process increased awareness of the system's internal and external dynamics so that future adaptations are enhanced."[2] Thus, the field is seen as all-inclusive, but with a unique organization/person orientation "directed toward integrating the needs, goals, and objectives of the organization with the needs of the individual for involvement, growth, and development on the job."[3]

The shift has been away from management development (MD) toward a broader view of employee development (ED), including any employee in any situation and all of the attitudinal, behavioral, procedural, policy, and structural variables which may affect him. Thus, whereas the historical model implied that organization development was management development (OD = MD), the new model implies that organization development is employee development (not restricted to a select group of employees) and much more (OD = ED + . . .). A systematic view of OD includes all "stakeholders" in the organization, especially when organizational boundaries are difficult to define.

The intent of this paper is to examine some of the specifics of employee participation (EP) within the OD model, to develop an analytical framework for the EP/OD processes, and to outline an action approach to EP. From the literature on participation, a number of assumptions appear critical:

1. that employees are "worth" developing (for the sake of the organization and/or for their own sake as human beings)
2. that employees are "capable" of being developed
3. that EP and OD are legitimate activities designed to move an organization into a more mature phase in its life cycle and
4. that since EP/OD implies that an organizaton's life cycle consists of a number of phases on a time continuum, the time dynamic must be considered in any EP/OD model.

THE DIMENSIONS OF EMPLOYEE PARTICIPATION IN OD

Implicit in much of the literature on OD is the notion of active participation by members of the organization, at least in that part of the organization on which the developmental focus lies.[4] While most references in North American literature on employee-level involvement in OD deal with managers and supervisors, the Western European experience includes more and more participation by employees at the lowest hierarchical level.[5] Thus, a comprehensive model of OD includes the full hierarchical spectrum of employees. The major focus of this paper is on supervisory and nonsupervisory employees toward the bottom of the hierarchy.

The important dimensions of employee participation in OD appear to include: (1) decisional participation; (2) decisional topic; (3) hierarchical level; (4) the time dynamic; and (5) the task. The model to be developed deals with the general class "employee," which is meant to include the nonsupervisory employee.

Decisional Participation

Judging by the Western European experience with employee participation, as well as by the discussion in the literature, there appear to be five degrees of decisional participation: (1) not being informed; (2) being informed; (3) being heard; (4) codetermining; and (5) totally determining. This dimension is essentially a function of the competence of the employee, as perceived by himself or herself and/or as perceived by his or her superior. Perception of competence, rather than objective competence, is the issue.

This distinction follows the pattern prescribed in the OD literature, which insists that perceptions and attitudes are at least as important as skills.

Employee participation implies a growth or movement from one side of a continuum toward the other (from "not being informed" to "totally determining"). It is obvious that in our culture the growing edge of this dimension is in the direction of determination, with the historical position being that employees are somewhere toward the other end of the continuum.

Decisional Topic

While the nature of the individual's task may call for relating it to others' tasks, both inside and outside his department, an individual frequently is interested in how his task contributes to a larger whole. To some degree, everyone participates with regard to his own job; but some people may, by their nature or by the nature of their task, also seek to participate in deciding how, when, or where their task interfaces with another. On that basis, it is possible to enumerate several decisional topics, in increasing scope: (1) the individual's job (tasks and working circumstances); (2) the individual's task group; (3) the individual's department; (4) other departments and interdepartmental issues, frequently including the personnel department; and (5) the organization.[6]

Assigning decisional topics to the above categories is in part subjective and arbitrary because some topics may fit into more than one. Nonetheless, this dimension and the previous one can be used in combination to examine the present state of an individual or group. Figure 1 allows for simultaneous consideration of the degree of participation and the decisional topic. Decisional participation is listed on the horizontal dimension and decisional topic on the vertical dimension.

Figure 1 shows that decisional participation in different decisional topics has different possible and acceptable ranges ("X" to "O") for nonsupervisory employees. The usefulness of a two-dimensional analysis may be contrasted with that of an analysis of worker decisional participation when the decisional topic is not specified. Even within a single decisional topic (such as the individual's own job) decisional participation may vary with the aspect of the topic. For example, one might claim a high decisional participation level for determining an optimum machine speed for a given product but might justify a low participation level for deciding on appropriate testing for determining progression through the job steps.

Decisional Participation → Decisional Topic ↓	1. Not being informed	2. Being informed	3. Being heard	4. Codetermining	5. Totally determining
a. Individual's job	X				O
b. Individual's task group	X				O
c. Individual's department	X			O	
d. Other departments	X		O		
e. The organization	X	O			

FIGURE 1
Example of Decisional Participation in Decisional Topics by Nonsupervisory Employees

In terms of specific cells of the matrix, a nonsupervisory employee might be rated as operating appropriately in cells 2a, 2b, 1c, 1d, and 1e, or possibly 3a, 2b, 1c, 1d, and 1e. By comparison, a low-level supervisory employee might be rated in cells 4a, 3b, 2c, 1d, and 1e. A member of the board of directors might be operating in cells 5a, 5b, 5c, 4d, and 4e. Such assumptions ignore the question of hierarchy, which introduces the third dimension of employee development.

Hierarchical Level

There are a number of hierarchical levels in most organizations. In this model, the following have been selected, in descending hierarchical order: (1) institutional (the board of directors, possibly including the chief executive officer); (2) presidential office (which might include vice-presidents of the major functional areas and general staff); (3) operating management; (4) supervisory employees (including foremen and assistant foremen); and (5) nonsupervisory employees.

If five organizational levels are considered, it is necessary to construct five separate decisional participation/decisional topic matrices to illustrate all combinations. An alternative is to attempt to construct a three-dimensional matrix such as that in Figure 2, which reflects five discrete levels in each of three dimensions. The axes represent decisional participation, decisional topic, and hierarchical level.

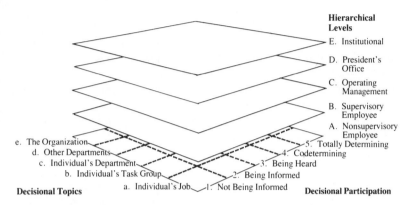

FIGURE 2
Decisional Topics, Decisional Participation, and Hierarchical Levels

The following degrees of decisional participation/decisional topic illustrate a possible distribution of these functions across levels of a hypothetical organization:

A. Nonsupervisory employee	3a, 2b, 1c, 1d, 1e
B. Supervisory employee	4a, 3b, 2c, 2d, 1e
C. Operating management	4a, 3b, 2c, 2d, 1e
D. President's office	4a, 4b, 3c, 2d, 2e
E. Institutional	5a, 5b, 5c, 4d, 4e

Time Dynamic

Up to this point, the model has not incorporated the time dimension — a dimension which provides opportunity for increasing decisional participation and topics and therefore appropriately increasing scope and/or degree of participation. The static picture of the organization as it is may be exchanged for one that anticipates more desirable conditions at a future time; that is, future states might be plotted on the model and attempts made (through employee development) to help people grow from present to future participatory states as their competence increases. Organization development is typically concerned with employee behavior (as a function of ability competence) in the future, typically one or more years from the present. It is possible in the multidimensional matrix to specify a goal for decisional participation/decisional topic for each hierarchical level.

For example, in a department where the existing situation might be defined as 2a, 2b, 1c, 1d, 1e, the goal over a five-year period might be to provide for greater decisional discretion or a higher degree of participation over more decisional topics. On the matrix, the goal might be defined as 4a, 3b, 3c, 2d, 2e. An explicit statement of position to which an individual (or level) must move makes it easier to select an appropriate course of action and to devote appropriate means to reaching that goal. Figure 3 expands this concept across the hierarchical dimension.

Hierarchical Level / Time Situations	1979 Situation	1984 Situation
A. Nonsupervisory employee	2a, 2b, 1c, 1d, 1e	4a, 4b, 2c, 2d, 2e
B. Supervisory employee	3a, 2b, 2c, 1d, 1e	4a, 4b, 3c, 3d, 3e
C. Operating management	4a, 3b, 2c, 2d, 2e	4a, 4b, 4c, 4d, 3e
D. President's office	5a, 4b, 3c, 4d, 5e	5a, 4b, 4c, 4d, 4e
E. Institutional	5a, 4b, 3c, 4d, 5e	5a, 4b, 4c, 4d, 4e

FIGURE 3
Example of Actual 1979 and 1984 Target Situations For
Various Hierarchical Levels

While Figure 3 may appear to imply that it is possible to specify a clearly defined goal for 1984 for each hierarchical level, this implication is not intended. Individuals and groups, both within and across hierarchical levels, differ greatly in the degree of their codetermination needs. Additionally, the process orientation of employee participation programs means that departments and/or groups should not be expected to achieve the same level of decisional maturity simultaneously.

Decisional maturity is a combination of the maturity of an individual's personality and his maturity with respect to the organization of which he is a member. Within the organization, the individual must first stabilize his organizational entity. As he becomes more aware of his goals and their relationship to organizational goals and demands, he becomes able to act with greater consistency in different decisional situations. Further, as personal relationships become freer, the individual becomes less self-conscious and less psychologically defensive about decisional actions. When the employee is less concerned about self he can spend more effort on being observant and responsive to the decisional situation. Finally, because the individual moves out along new paths, his interest is likely to deepen, he becomes absorbed in his work, and he desires to see end results of his contributions. This change is related to a growth of competence and of motivation to achieve. Thus, the neophyte member of the organization, unfamiliar with all of its ways, reluctant to make any kind of decisional move, matures into a contributing member who has identified his role in the organization and is ready to take on successive new challenges.[7]

With this organizational membership maturation process, situations may be viewed by the member as decisionally deprived (participation in fewer decisions than desired) or decisionally saturated (participation in greater number of decisions than desired).[8] A balanced condition is referred to s decisional equilibrium.

Within the process orientation of employee participation programs there is an unavoidable disturbance of the decisional equilibrium of participants, possibly caused initially by a deprivation situation and resulting in a saturation situation. Empirical reports of long-term decisional saturation or deprivation and their symptoms are not evident in the management literature.

Task

The foregoing discussion has developed four dimensions of employee participation processes: decisional participation, decisional topic, hierarchical level, and the time dynamic. Additional dimensions may be introduced; however, only one will be added here. Many textbooks on management principles discuss the major managerial functions, which may be summarized as: planning, organizing, executing, and controlling. These are pertinent functions for every level in an organization, even for nonsupervisory employees. They are important functions for one's own work, and also for seeing that the work of lower levels is implemented. Thus, it is appropriate for even the nonsupervisory employee to plan (formulate explicit goals and objectives related to his task and its contribution to organizational goals), organize (choose from among alternative means of completing that task), execute, and control his own work.

This fifth dimension can be added to the previous ones, but since drawing either a four- or five-dimensional figure is not possible, an example will have to suffice for purposes of illustration. Consider a situation for nonsupervisory employees, with regard to their own departments, where the situation might be defined as 1I, 2II, 3III, 1IV, as illustrated in the following matrix (Figure 4). The "X" in the cells represents the existing situation, and the "O" represents a desired level of participation at a future date.

Task / Decisional Participation	I Plan	II Organize	III Execute	IV Control
1. Not being informed	X			X
		X	X	
3. Being heard	O			
4. Codetermining		O	O	O
5. Totally determining				

FIGURE 4
Example of Existing (X) and Future (O) Decisional Participation in Tasks by Nonsupervisory Employees

CONCLUSION

It is argued that the philosophy underlying the development of managers is applicable to the development of all of an organization's human resources, and that an organization ought to utilize organization development strategies for the development of all its employees. To approach this problem rationally, it is first necessary to know the current status of the organization's members. The next step is to determine the level(s) to which they should be developed at a future date. Action programs are then required to move people from their current status to the future desired state. The preceding model provides a structure for evaluation and decision making with emphasis on participation, a key ingredient of the organization development philosophy.

FOOTNOTES

1. R. Beckhard, *Organization Development: Strategies and Models* (Reading, Mass.: Addison-Wesley Publishing Company, 1969).

2. R.E. Miles, *Theories of Management: Implications for Organizational Behavior and Development* (New York: McGraw-Hill Book Company, 1975), p. 191.

3. F. Huse and J.F. Bowditch, *Behavior in Organizations: A Systems Approach to Managing* (Reading, Mass.: Addison-Wesley Publishing Company, 1977), p. 386.

4. H.J. Leavitt, "Applied Organizational Change in Industry," in *Contingency Views of Organization and Management,* eds. F.E. Kast and J.E. Rosenzweig (Chicago: Science Research Associates, Inc., 1973), pp. 57-73; D.M. McGregor, "The Human Side of Enterprise," in *Contemporary Readings in Organizational Behavior,* ed. F. Luthans (New York: McGraw-Hill Book Company, 1972), pp. 31-40; L.W. Porter, E.E. Lawler III, and J.R. Hackman, *Behavior in Organizations* (New York: McGraw-Hill Book Company, 1975); A. Tannenbaum, *Control in Organizations* (New York: McGraw-Hill Book Company, 1968).

5. H.J. van Dongen, "Organization Development and Participation," in *Labor and Organization Psychology,* eds. Drenth, Willems and de Wolf (Deventer: Kluwer, 1973), pp. 295-96; J. Herrema, "Experiences with Shop Council Programs," *Ondernemen* (June-July 1972); J.H. Kuipers, *Management Through a Shop Council Program* (Alphen a/d Rijn: Samson Uitgeverij, 1973); J.G. Scheurer, "Shop Council Programs," in *Informatief* No. 8: Bureaucracy, Democratization of Shop Council Pro-

grams (Scheveningen: Stichting Maatschappij en Onderneming, 1974); Shop Council Committee, Noord Brabant, *Shop Council Program in Practice* (The Hague: NIVE, 1972); L.P. Sikkel, "Shop Council Programs: The Inevitability," *T.E.D.* (January 1974); J. Vermeulen, "Shop Council Programs: What, Why, How?" *Ondernemen* 29 (June-July 1973).

6. G.R.M. Scholten, *Participation and Organizational Change* (The Hague: Rapport C.O.P./S.E.R., 1975). Scholten has reported on "topics of interest" and "topics discussed" in worker participation programs at the nonsupervisory level. When categorized according to a scheme similar to that described here, frequencies of responses were as follows: individual's job, 37; individual's department, 13; other departments, 6.

7. D.A. Kimmel, *Adulthood: An Interdisciplinary Developmental Model* (New York: John Wiley & Sons, 1973); Carl A. Rogers, *On Becoming a Person* (Boston: Houghton Mifflin Company, 1961); R.W. White, *Lives in Progress* (New York: Holt, Rinehart & Winston, 1952).

8. J.A. Aluto and J.A. Belasco, "A Typology for Participation in Organizational Decision Making," *Administrative Science Quarterly* 17 (March 1972).

REFERENCES

Aluto, J.A., and Belasco, J.A. "A Typology for Participation in Organizational Decision Making." *Administrative Science Quarterly* 17 (March 1972).

Beckhard, R. *Organization Development: Strategies and Models*. Reading, Mass.: Addison-Wesley Publishing Company, 1969.

Dongen, van, H.J. "Organization Development and Participation." In *Labor and Organization Psychology*. Edited by Drenth, Willems and de Wolf. Deventer: Kluwer, 1973.

Herrema, J. "Experiences with Shop Council Programs." *Ondernemen* (June-July 1972).

Huse, F., and Bowditch, J.F. *Behavior in Organizations: A Systems Approach to Managing*. Reading, Mass.: Addison-Wesley Publishing Company, 1977.

Kimmel, D.A. *Adulthood: An Interdisciplinary Developmental Model*. New York: John Wiley & Sons, 1973.

Kuipers, J.H. *Management Through a Shop Council Program*. Alphen a/d Rijn: Samson Uitgeverij, 1973.

Leavitt, H.J. "Applied Organizational Change in Industry." In *Contingency Views of Organization and Management*. Edited by F.E. Kast and J.E. Rosenzweig. Chicago: Science Research Associates, Inc., 1973.

McGregor, D.M. "The Human Side of Enterprise." In *Contemporary Readings in Organizational Behavior*. Edited by F. Luthans. New York: McGraw-Hill Book Company, 1972.

Miles, R.E. *Theories of Management: Implications for Organizational Behavior and Development*. New York: McGraw-Hill Book Company, 1975.

Porter, L.W.; Lawler, E.E. III; and Hackman, J.R. *Behavior in Organizations*. New York: McGraw-Hill Book Company, 1975.

Rogers, Carl A. *On Becoming a Person*. Boston: Houghton Mifflin Company, 1961.

Scheurer, J.G. "Shop Council Programs," In *Informatief* No. 8: Bureaucracy, Democratization of Shop Council Programs. Scheveningen: Stichting Maatschappij en Onderneming, 1974.

Scholten, G.R.M. *Participation and Organizational Change*. The Hague: Rapport C.O.P./S.E.R., 1975.

Shop Council Committee, Noord Brabant.*Shop Council Program in Practice*. The Hague: NIVE, 1972.

Sikkel, L.P. "Shop Council Programs: The Inevitability." *T.E.D.* (January 1974).

Tannenbaum, A. *Control in Organizations*. New York: McGraw-Hill Book Company, 1968.

Vermeulen, J. "Shop Council Programs: What, Why, How?" *Ondernemen* 29 (June-July 1973).

White, R.W. *Lives in Progress*. New York: Holt, Rinehart & Winston, 1952.

GUIDELINES FOR THE MANAGEMENT OF TEMPORARY TASK FORCE TEAMS

Sandra L. Gill

Although the utilization of professional and lay planning groups in innovative program development has become commonplace in human service organizations, seldom are emergent or assigned group leaders given training in group management. Group leadership skills usually are assumed to accompany the technical/professional expertise which brings these people to the leadership circle. The costs of this assumption are clearly reflected in the problems encountered by task force teams which lack adequate group facilitation.

Whether formally or informally developed, groups are ubiquitous in organizational life.[1] However, the need for group leadership skills is especially critical in the case of a temporary or *ad hoc* planning task force or team. Complex innovative planning efforts are a special case of program management requiring strategic inter- and intra-group facilitation.[2] Where the problem or mission is not well understood or where solution strategies require an approach which is not routine, the group leader must deal with the special demands created by factors of innovation.[3] Hence under the dual conditions of: (1) a complex planning goal requiring innovation and (2) a group decision-making body as the planning unit, group leaders must focus on both the achievement of the steps in the planning cycle and the facilitation of the planning team's development.

The demands of innovative planning include, but are not limited to, the acquisition of a clear, firm mandate for a further exploration of the planning issue based on the multiple levels of organizational interest; the establishment of a representative review body to provide the planning team with feedback and strategic authorization during the planning effort; and periodic well-structured decision and review procedures for planning tasks.

The purpose of this paper is to synthesize relevant literature and to suggest behavioral guidelines for effective group leadership of temporary project or planning task forces created to lead innovative program planning efforts. The assumptions are:

1. that an effective planning effort for an innovative project is pre-requisite to the effective functioning and development of the planning group or task force, and

2. that successful management of such groups will be enhanced by leadership response to two sets of issues concerning the planning team — i.e., those which precede official group formation and those which parallel group development.

LEADERSHIP FOR GROUP FORMATION

Conditions for Group Formation

According to the literature on small groups, under certain circumstances group efforts may have results superior to those of individual efforts. If a leader is sensitive to these circumstances, he or she can use diagnostic guidelines to match his or her goal to the potential of the planning team. Knowing when to use a group instead of individuals enables the leader to maximize group resources. Knowing when *not* to use a group can prevent unnecessary frustrations.

The most obvious benefit of group effort is the increase in resources, which allows for both a division of labor[4] and increased technical skills.[5] A group also can provide a variety of cognitive resources for problem solving:

1. increase in the number of items of information that can be absorbed and recalled
2. increase in the number of critical judgments available to correct errors in inference and analysis
3. increase in the number of suggested solution strategies
4. increase in attention to the task because of social facilitation, i.e., individuals tend to apply themselves more diligently to a task given the presence of others in the immediate situation.[6]

Thus, needs for a division of labor, for increased technical skills, and for cognitive resources from a variety of individual backgrounds are primary indicators that a group effort is appropriate.

The nature of the planning project is another clue to the need for a group. The use of a group is appropriate when the planning solution or strategy is undetermined and requires creative pooled judgment. The use of individuals is appropriate when routine analysis and the application of available expertise are involved.[7] The need to coordinate multiple technical areas or jurisdictions, as opposed to the need to implement routine, single-unit technology, calls for group planning.[8] The inclusion of multiple disciplines, perspectives, and specialized information, where there is shared interest in the problem, is facilitated through group planning efforts.[9] In short, where a planning effort has no known precedent and requires a creative, judgmental design, a group planning team is appropriate.

Group Cohesion

Cohesion does not result automatically from group interaction. A cohesive group can be characterized by a shared sense of attraction of its members to the group.[10] Such groups offer certain benefits: (1) beneficial and responsible group activity; (2) interpersonal attention, acceptance, and listening; (3) member support and protection of group goals; and (4) release of tension.[11] However, there is also a tendency toward group think, where members sacrifice their individual opinions.[12]

To achieve cohesion, the group manager must consider the risks associated with group membership and must carefully guide the group's development. First, at the individual level, temporary project group members face significant uncertainties about their re-entry to their full-time "home base": (1) fear of obsolescence following removal from their technical/professional core groups; (2) concern about the consequences of being absent in relation to long-run promotions should the problem at hand not be directly applicable to upward mobility in their full-time positions; (3) uncertainty about future assignments: "Will my spot be filled? Will I be given less important tasks on my return? Will the project fail and affect my career?"; and (4) concern about work overload as a consequence of assuming a split-time appointment.[13]

The group leader's response to these concerns begins with negotiations with the supervisor of the prospective group member before official assignment to the group occurs. At this time, re-entry concerns can be safely articulated and procedures for rewarding services rendered to the project team can be planned. Simultaneously, the conditions of the member's return can be clarified so that the participant and whoever assumes his tasks in absentia share an understanding of the re-entry stage.

Communicating results of these negotiations to group members gives the leader an opportunity to respond to additional questions about group membership. The articulation of goals and potential objectives for the planning team can be an opportunity to defuse members' concern about being overburdened by excessive group demands.[14] In addition to specifying tasks to be accomplished, probable frequency of group meetings, and length of group membership, the leader should inform members that the group will maintain a problem-solving orientation in which each member's insight will be valued, rather than a win-lose, majority-rule mode of forced decisions. Furthermore, because members frequently disagree on the problem-solving method, [15] the leader will be strengthened by the command of a repertoire of problem-solving strategies, especially in the area of managing dominating personalities [16] and negative evaluations. [17]

Of direct value to the individual member is a group's opportunity to increase its members' prestige. [18] This factor re-emphasizes the need for the leader to have a full understanding of the project's mandate and organizational significance. Additional sources of attraction for members include the opportunity to work in a more flexible or experimental environment [19] and with a smaller, more personal group. [20]

At the group level, leaders must be aware that project teams need to develop sufficient cohesion for task achievement but also to remain open to the concerns of the larger organization in which they function. Once individual concerns are resolved, project teams should coalesce as a result of sharing perceptions and a sense of the task at hand. [21] While identification of problems is a potent force for the group's short-run development, in the long run the project group members will re-enter the larger organization and the product or plan must be accepted by diverse and more distant colleagues and constituents. This dual goal — to develop a cohesive task group while preserving its responsiveness to a larger organization — requires special leadership efforts to achieve an effective yet flexible working mode.

Strategies which demonstrate the relationship of the planning team and its efforts to organizational goals, sub-unit objectives, and members' personal interests are essential. [22] Leaders must be able to articulate, both within and beyond the group boundary, congruence of the team with other units without sacrificing the team's special, time-specific focus. (This task hopefully would be undertaken by group members as well.) The overall framework and authority structure by which the planning team relates to ongoing organizational operations should be demonstrated, particularly where there is an opportunity to show linkage with groups that have been successful in the past. [23]

The group's effort eventually will be transferred back to a larger organizational set. Agreement on the timing and format of communication to personnel who authorize members' released time or reassignment offers an opportunity to build good working relations. Identifying key decision makers and acquainting them with the team's history and the anticipated outcome of its efforts will be a critical liaison role for the group leader. The project group may come to view itself as the only source of relevant expertise and be resistant to external input. In this case, the leader and the group members will benefit from the use of problem-solving and negotiating skills to gather and incorporate into the planning effort important perceptions of individuals and groups external to the task force team. The leader must be able to depersonalize important perceptions expressed by individuals or groups within the task force in order to promote group discussion of ideas rather than a "we-they" debate of personalities.

The impact of group size on group functioning merits special consideration by group leaders. Because the details of this phenomenon have been carefully detailed elsewhere,[24] the differential outcomes and implications for leadership will be only summarized here. First, an increase in the number of group members affects the content, the emotional involvement among group members, and the distribution of members' interaction.[25] In general, groups with more than seven members experience fewer attempts than smaller groups to clarify and seek out opinions, receive more "pronouncements" from high-status members, and have a tendency toward unresolved conflicts. Power plays replace problem solving, threat of negative reactions inhibits involvement, and activists assume greater control. The group dissolves into smaller subgroups and cohesion is lost.

To maintain the benefits of group membership, the effective leader must employ a variety of problem-solving and decision-making procedures which take into consideration the different characteristics of various-sized groups along with the nature of the issue at hand. A planning issue may easily have several components. One component may be simply the sharing of relevant facts among group members. This kind of sharing lends itself to a dyadic exchange between the "expert" and the rest of the group. Another component may be the generating of relevant creative ideas by encouraging individual, noninteractive participation without passing judgment. Brainstorming and the nominal group technique (NGT) can be useful strategies for identifying problems and designing solutions.[26] Issues for which no known solution exists can be explored through small structured group processes which combine individual thoughts with group judgment, e.g., force field analyses[27] and NGT. Decisions regarding an ultimate solution strategy will be enhanced by the inclusion of many individual perspectives, subject to group consensus, e.g., functional analysis[28] and estimate-talk-estimate procedures.[29]

In short, accomplishment of a planning task is influenced by the decision-making mode, which is significantly determined by the size of the group. The dual demands of making decisions and maintaining group attraction require that the leader be sensitive to the influences of group size and have a command of a variety of decision-making processes.

In summary, the group leader has critical responsibilities preceding official group formation. First, he must determine whether the nature of the planning task is suited to a group effort. Does it require analysis or judgment? Can needed resources be acquired by administrative authority or must they be requested on the basis of cooperation? Will the effort demand procedures which are already routine or will it affect multiple jurisdictions of previously unassociated personnel? Affirmative responses to the second parts of these questions suggest the need for group effort.

Second, cohesive groups can stimulate individual productivity.[30] A group leader can enhance this perceived attraction of the group by minimizing membership risks before official assignments are made. The dual leadership role here is that of (1) a problem-solving negotiator to clarify conditions of group membership and develop agreed upon procedures for ensuring each member's comfortable re-entry to his professional/technical core upon the project group's termination; (2) a facilitator of project transfer at the completion of the planning team's task, and of group sensitivity to ongoing organizational perceptions.

With these matters resolved, proactive rather than reactive leadership can be directed to the second set of concerns, those associated directly with the stages of group development.

LEADERSHIP FOR
GROUP DEVELOPMENT

Small group developmental studies leave much to be desired in terms of their representation of natural groups, their validity, and their scientific rigor.[31] Tuckman has provided an overall conceptual model derived from the results of a variety of group studies.[32] This is a developmental model — i.e., it describes generic changes within groups over time. According to this model, group leadership needs are dynamic rather than static; one's leadership orientation therefore should be "different ways on different days."[33]

In the first stage of group life *(forming),* members expect task orientation from their leader.[34] The central concerns are to define what is to be accomplished and how it is to be accomplished. This definition usually occurs through testing — i.e., attempting to discover, through the reactions of the leader and other group members, what behaviors are acceptable and what information is needed. Group members expect guidance and support from the leader in structuring this new situation.

In the absence of such leadership, other forces will fill this vacuum. Individuals who discover common values, who have similar personalities, and who originate from proximate social or work-related circles are destined toward social cohesion.[35] Furthermore, these factors create a relatively stable pattern of interaction.[36] Regardless of the basis of group formation, however, the stability of the group and its continuance are secure only if shared values or interests are present or evolve.[37] In other words, the group leader must focus on task achievement, in order to link members through a common task-oriented purpose. Congruence of personalities within the group will facilitate the sharing of expertise, and frequent task-related interaction may lead to new social relations.[38]

The group leader's orientation to the role of the planning group provides an opportunity to restate and explore: (1) the relationship of the planning group to the organizational goals; (2) planning objectives in broad terms (allowing for modification by the group); (3) timing and format of feedback, relative to task achievements; and (4) termination, project transfer, and member re-entry procedures.

The leader should explain not only his commitment to a group problem-solving mode using a repertoire of group processes but also the likelihood of varying demands on members' expertise during the planning effort.[39] Finally, because effective groups demand both task-instrumental and socio-emotional leadership, the importance of both kinds of involvement and their potential contribution to the group should be stated.[40]

Soon after the group's formation, the second stage of its development *(storming)* begins as the novelty of the new group recedes in the face of the task's reality. A leadership struggle may emerge in which individual members attempt to secure authority. There may be serious disagreement over conservative vs. risky strategies for group task achievement. While the degree of disharmony varies, almost all small-group studies examined by Tuckman demonstrated more disruption in this second stage than in the initial stage.

The presence of such conflict need not be disadvantageous. Filley has suggested certain advantages to conflict situations: (1) tension may stimulate problem solving and the search for new facts, if the conflict can be focused on issues rather than on the people involved; (2) the presence of conflict can offer an early opportunity for group decision making; and (3) the potential exists for increased cohesion through the use of methods resulting in mutual gain ("win/win" conflict resolution strategies). [41]

At this point, the leader's role shifts to that of a statesperson who facilitates problem-solving processes, [42] who acknowledges personal concerns and, if necessary, gives them an issue orientation through, e.g., active listening [43] and feedback rules. [44] Aspects of this role include emphasizing description rather than judgment of concerns and specific rather than general or ambiguous statements of events; focusing on changeable rather than solidified matters; being concerned with present rather than unalterable past occurrences; and protecting minority opinions.

Two behavioral patterns to be avoided during conflict are dyadic leader-member interaction patterns and reliance on parliamentary democracy. Dyadic conflict resolution strategies often lead to power-invoked resolution and persistent desires by the "loser" to "get even". Parliamentary procedures which begin with a motion or proposal suggest a conclusion rather than a careful exploration of the issue. [45] Both strategies repress dissent.

If conflict is carefully managed, rules and group standards can be established which lead to the third stage of the group life cycle *(norming)*. The security of roles and rules provides an opportunity for full application of member expertise, provided the group leader adheres to agreed upon standards. An acceptable style of feedback can be designed to reinforce members' sense of responsibility to their assigned tasks. At this time, the leader needs to be especially skillful in managing decision making, so that each member maintains an active, interested role, undiminished by the results of hasty judgments or the influence of powerful personalities. The leader must be able to articulate the benefits to the group of solidarity and to provide norms to prevent suboptimization.

Finally, after achieving interpersonal security and functional roles sufficient for task achievement, the group enters its fourth stage *(performing)*. At this time, a weary leader may retreat into the comfort of his technical/professional role instead of maintaining leadership performance. [46] However, a balanced response to the demands of coordination and those of participation as an expert is required for task achievement and member maintenance. A leader must maintain a schedule through frequent communication with the group and awareness of its independent effort. This proactive position allows: (1) adjustments prior to crisis; (2) problem solving rather than crisis-demanded, solitary decision making; and (3) opportunities to preserve group attraction through the use of rewards rather than sanctions.

In summary, effective group leadership demands much more than intuition, social grace, and task efficiency. A group leader must be sensitive to the needs of group members as individuals and as organizational representatives, and have technical familiarity with the task to be accomplished. To prevent decision-making failure and consequent group dissatisfaction, he must possess a repertoire of decision-making skills. Because groups typically go through a series of developmental stages, leadership must be proactive and responsive. The leader must have a combination of analytic, diagnostic, prescriptive, and interpersonal skills.

While it is highly unlikely that one person will command all of these skills, it is reasonable to expect that group functioning will improve if attention is given to them.[47] Training for task force leadership thus constitutes a significant yet apparently unmet need in the preparation of human service professionals and offers a profitable area for interdisciplinary applied research.

FOOTNOTES

1. Fremont Shull, Jr., A.L. Delbecq, and L.L. Cummings, eds., *Organizational Decisionmaking* (New York: McGraw-Hill Book Company, 1970); B.B. Gardner, "What Makes Successful and Unsuccessful Managers?" *Advanced Management* 13 (Sept. 1948): 116-24.

2. A.L. Delbecq, A.H. Van de Ven, and D.H. Gustafson, *Group Techniques for Program Planning: A Guide to Nominal Group and Delphi Processes* (Glenview, Ill.: Scott, Foresman and Company, 1975).

3. P.R. Lawrence and J.W. Lorsch, *Organization and Environment* (Boston: Division of Research, Harvard Business School, 1967), p. 145; A.L. Delbecq and A.C. Filley, *Program and Project Management in a Matrix Organization: A Case Study* (University of Wisconsin, Bureau of Business Research, 1974), p. 20.

4. John Cohen, "Social Thinking," *Acta Psychologica* 9 (1953): 146-58.

5. Shull *et al.*, 1970.

6. Ibid.

7. H.H. Kelley and J.W. Thibaut, "Experimental Studies of Group Problem Solving and Process," in *Handbook of Social Psychology*, Vol. II, ed. G. Lindzey (Reading, Mass.: Addison-Wesley Publishing Company, 1954), pp. 735-85; A.P. Hare, *Handbook of Small Group Research*, 2nd ed. (New York: The Free Press, 1976), pp. 318-25.

8. A.H. Van de Ven and A.L. Delbecq, "A Planning Process for Development of Complex Regional Programs," paper delivered at the 67th Annual Meeting of the American Sociological Association, New Orleans, Louisiana, August 1972, pp 2-3.

9. A.L. Delbecq *et al.*, 1975.

10. D. Cartwright and A. Zander, eds., *Group Dynamics: Research and Theory* (New York: Row, Peterson and Company, 1960), p. 72.

11. Ibid., pp. 69-94.

12. I.L. Janis, *Victims of Groupthink* (Boston: Houghton-Mifflin Co., 1972), pp. 2-13.

13. Delbecq and Filley, 1974, pp. 62-66.

14. E. Stotland, "Determinants of Attraction to Groups," *The Journal of Social Psychology* 49 (1959): 71-80.

15. J.R.P. French, Jr., "The Disruption and Cohesion of Groups," *Journal of Abnormal and Social Psychology* 36 (1941): 361-77.

16. N. Fouriezos, M. Hutt, and H. Guetzkow, "Measurement of Self-Oriented Needs in Discussion Groups," *Journal of Abnormal and Social Psychology* 45 (1950): 682-90.

17. A. Davis, B. Gardner, and M. Gardner, *Deep South: A Social and Anthropological Study of Caste and Class* (Chicago: University of Chicago Press, 1941).

18. H.H. Kelley, "Communication in Experimentally Created Hierarchies," in Cartwright and Zander, 1960, pp. 781-99.

19. Delbecq and Filley, 1974, p. 60.

20. J. Tsouderos, "Organizational Change in Terms of a Series of Selected Variables," *American Sociological Review* 20 (1955): 207-10.

21. T.M. Newcomb, "Varieties of Interpersonal Attraction," in Cartwright and Zander, 1960, pp. 104-19.

22. J. Dittes, "Attractiveness of Group as a Function of Self-Esteem and Acceptance by Group," *Journal of Abnormal and Social Psychology* 59 (1959): 77-82.

23. Stotland, 1959; S. Seashore, *Group Cohesiveness in the Industrial Work Group* (Ann Arbor, Michigan: Institute for Social Research, 1954).

24. Shull *et al.,* 1970; A.L. Delbecq, "The World Within the 'Span of Control'," *Business Horizons* (August 1968): 47-56.

25. Delbecq, 1968.

26. Hare, 1976, pp. 318-25.

27. Edgard F. Huse, *Organization Development and Change* (St. Paul: West Publishing Company, 1975), pp. 48-52.

28. Lawrence D. Miles, *Techniques of Value Analysis and Engineering* (New York: McGraw-Hill, 1972).

29. D.H. Gustafson *et al.,* "A Comparative Study of Differences in Subjective Likelihood Estimates Mode by Individuals, Interacting Groups, Delphi Groups, and Nominal Groups" (Madison, Wisc.: University of Wisconsin, Department of Industrial Engineering, 1971.

30. Cartwright and Zander, 1960, p. 92.

31. B.W. Tuckman, "Developmental Sequence in Small Groups," *Psychological Bulletin* 63 (1965): 384-99.

32. Ibid.

33. E. Hammer, "Keynote address to the Mt. Plains Regional Center for Services to Deaf-Blind Children," Santa Fe, New Mexico, 1973.

34. Tuckman, 1965; Shull *et al.,* 1970.

35. Cartwright and Zander, 1960; A.P. Hare, *Handbook of Small Group Research* (Glencoe, Ill.: Free Press, 1962), pp. 318-25.

36. Shull *et al.,* 1970.

37. Newcomb, 1960; E.O. Laumann, in Shull *et. al.,* 1970, p. 132.

38. G.C. Homans, *The Human Group* (New York: Harcourt, Brace & World, Inc., 1950), pp. 34-40.

39. Delbecq and Filley, 1974.

40. Shull *et al.,* 1970.

41. A.C. Filley, *Interpersonal Conflict Resolution* (Glenview, Ill.: Scott, Foresman and Company, 1975), pp. 4-7.

42. Lawrence and Lorsch, 1967.

43. T. Gordon, *Parent Effectiveness Training* (New York: David McKay Co., 1970).

44. Filley, 1975, pp. 41-43.

45. N.R.F. Maier, *Problem Solving Discussions and Conferences* (New York: McGraw-Hill Book Company, 1963).

46. Delbecq and Filley, 1974.

47. Kelley and Thibaut, 1954.

REFERENCES

Cartwright, D., and Zander, A., eds. *Group Dynamics: Research and Theory*. New York: Row, Peterson and Company, 1960.

Cohen, John. "Social Thinking." *Acta Psychologica* 9 (1953): 146-58.

Davis, A.; Gardner, B.; and Gardner, M. *Deep South: A Social and Anthropological Study of Caste and Class*. Chicago: University of Chicago Press, 1941.

Delbecq, A.L. "The World Within the 'Span of Control'." *Business Horizons* (August 1968): 47-56.

Delbecq, A.L., and Filley, A.C. *Program and Project Management in a Matrix Organization: A Case Study*. University of Wisconsin, Bureau of Business Research, 1974.

Delbecq, A.L.; Van de Ven, A.H.; and Gustafson, D.H. *Group Techniques for Program Planning: A Guide to Nominal Group and Delphi Processes*. Glenview, Ill.: Scott, Foresman and Company, 1975.

Dittes, J. "Attractiveness of Group as a Function of Self-Esteem and Acceptance by Group." *Journal of Abnormal and Social Psychology* 59 (1959): 77-82.

Filley, A.C. *Interpersonal Conflict Resolution*. Glenview, Ill.: Scott, Foresman and Company, 1975.

Fouriezos, N.; Hutt, M.; and Guetzkow, H. "Measurement of Self-Oriented Needs in Discussion Groups," *Journal of Abnormal and Social Psychology* 45 (1950): 682-90.

French, J.R.P., Jr. "The Disruption and Cohesion of Groups." *Journal of Abnormal and Social Psychology* 36 (1941): 361-77.

Gardner, B.B. "What Makes Successful and Unsuccessful Managers?" *Advanced Management* 13 (September 1948): 116-24.

Gordon, T. *Parent Effectiveness Training*. New York: David McKay Co., 1970.

Gustafson, D.H.; Shulka, R.K.; Delbecq, A.L.; and Walster, G.W. "A Comparative Study of Differences in Subjective Likelihood Estimates Mode by Individuals, Interacting Groups, Delphi Groups, and Nominal Groups." Madison, Wisc.: University of Wisconsin, Department of Industrial Engineering, 1971.

Hammer, E. "Keynote address to the Mt. Plains Regional Center for Services to Deaf-Blind Children." Santa Fe, New Mexico, 1973.

Hare, A. Paul. *Handbook of Small Group Research*. Glencoe, Ill.: Free Press, 1962.

Hare, A. Paul. *Handbook of Small Group Research*. 2nd ed. New York: The Free Press, 1976.

Homans, G.C. *The Human Group*. New York: Harcourt, Brace & World, Inc., 1950.

Huse, Edgard F. *Organization Development and Change*. St. Paul: West Publishing Company, 1975.

Janis, I.L. *Victims of Groupthink*. Boston: Houghton-Mifflin Co., 1972.

Kelley, H.H. "Communication in Experimentally Created Hierarchies." In *Group Dynamics: Research and Theory,* pp. 781-99. Edited by D. Cartwright and A. Zander. New York: Row, Peterson and Company, 1960.

Kelley, H.H., and Thibaut, J.W. "Experimental Studies of Group Problem Solving and Process." In *Handbook of Social Psychology,* Vol. II, pp. 735-85. Edited by G. Lindzey. Reading, Mass.: Addison-Wesley Publishing Company, 1954.

Laumann, E.O. In *Organizational Decisionmaking,* p. 132. Edited by Fremont Shull, Jr., A.L. Delbecq, and L.L. Cummings. New York: McGraw-Hill Book Company, 1970.

Lawrence, P.R., and Lorsch, J.W. *Organization and Environment.* Boston: Divison of Research, Harvard Business School, 1967.

Maier, N.R.F. *Problem Solving Discussions and Conferences.* New York: McGraw-Hill Book Company, 1963.

Miles, Lawrence D. *Techniques of Value Analysis and Engineering.* New York: McGraw-Hill, 1972.

Newcomb, T.M. "Varieties of Interpersonal Attraction." In *Group Dynamics: Research and Theory,* pp. 104-19. Edited by D. Cartwright and A. Zander. New York: Row, Peterson and Company, 1960.

Seashore, S. *Group Cohesiveness in the Industrial Work Group.* Ann Arbor, Michigan: Institute for Social Research, 1954.

Shull, Fremont, Jr.; Delbecq, A.L.; and Cummings, L.L. *Organizational Decisionmaking.* New York: McGraw-Hill Book Company, 1970.

Stotland, E. "Determinants of Attraction to Groups." *The Journal of Social Psychology* 49 (1959): 71-80.

Tsouderos, J. "Organizational Change in Terms of a Series of Selected Variables." *American Sociological Review 20* (1955): 207-10.

Tuckman, B.W. "Developmental Sequence in Small Groups." *Psychological Bulletin* 63 (1965): 384-99.

Van de Ven, A.H., and Delbecq, A.L. "A Planning Process for Development of Complex Regional Programs." Paper delivered at the 67th Annual Meeting of the American Sociological Association, New Orleans, Louisiana, August 1972.

NEGOTIATING A WORKING AGREEMENT

Louis A. Ferman

Human service administrators are becoming increasingly aware of the need for working relationships between their agencies and corporate organizations in the private sector. Corporate organizations are beginning to make more use of public and private agencies to treat "troubled" workers, to recruit workers, to train new work recruits, and to provide other supportive services. A sharp increase in the number of these relationships will occur, but not without problems, since there are differences between human service agencies and companies. Because these differences will influence the development of working agreements between the two types of organization, negotiations behavior will assume an important role in this process.

It must be recognized that all relationships between the agency and the company are the results of bargaining and negotiations. An important element, therefore, in agency operations is the existence of personnel who are, or can be trained to be, skilled bargainers and negotiators and who have the resources to make their work effective.

Negotiating an agreement requires a number of meetings to solicit a general policy mandate from the company and translate it into the specific provisions of a working agreement. In a typical case of negotiation, both sides seek to realize certain objectives and both sides make concessions. The agency may obtain a commitment for fewer services than it desired to give or the company may agree to take services under conditions that are not completely to its liking. In setting the limits of these concessions and recognizing the limits that can be set by the company, much skill is required of agency negotiators.

Negotiation is more than verbal interchange. It is a process that unfolds from a stage in which preparations are made to a stage in which the specific wording of the agreement is worked out. In the earliest stage the agency seeks a "yes or no" decision, i.e., the company is either willing or unwilling to avail itself of the services offered. At an intermediate stage, the agency seeks a decision on which of a number of service plans is acceptable to the company. At a later stage, the agency and company seek a common understanding of the language and provisions of the agreement.

A basic premise underlying all bargaining and negotiations between agency and company personnel is that effective communication can be translated into effective working arrangements between the organizations represented. Without bargaining skills, communication between the organizations can occur but cannot result in effective working relationships.

THE NEED FOR A NEGOTIATED AGREEMENT

The negotiation of an agreement between an agency and a company fulfills several important purposes:

1. The process of negotiation involves an ongoing interchange between agency and company personnel that sharpens the goals, objectives, and interests of each party. It also highlights the difficulties that must be overcome if the goals and objectives are to be achieved. Both parties probe the mutual expectations of an agency-company service program. The negotiation process is an educational and an information-gathering experience for both sides.

2. The negotiation of an agreement provides an opportunity to present alternative service plans as well as to adapt a given service plan to the realities of the company situation. The negotiation process forces agency personnel to think through their program and services in greater detail and to modify them if necessary.

3. The agreement itself, particularly in its written form, specifies what information, personnel, and resources will be required for the working relationships. It is a document that states who, where, and what, enabling both sides to engage in planning, assignment of personnel, and allocation of resources. In the absence of such a document, there is a high degree of uncertainty and unpredictability about the content of the agency program, how it is to be delivered, and who has major responsibilities.

4. Although the written agreement frequently has no legal standing, it does imply a moral commitment on the part of both agency and company personnel. It can be construed by the agency as a "license to operate."

These observations suggest a number of reasons for the extreme importance of a negotiated agreement. There are three operational principles that should underlie the development of such an agreement:

1. The agreement should be committed to writing. This procedure provides not only a documented set of guidelines for service operations but also a stronger expression of company commitment than a "handshake agreement."

2. The written agreement should be circulated widely and given exposure in the mass media to reinforce the commitment made by the company and demonstrate to other companies and agencies what is possible.

3. The written agreement should be reviewed periodically by both agency and company personnel to see if new services offered by the agency or new operating realities within the company have made revisions necessary. For example, a new counseling program may strengthen existing services of the agency; changes in the labor market may create a demand on the part of the company for new services.

THE CONTENT OF A NEGOTIATED AGREEMENT

The exact details of an agreement will, of course, vary from one situation to another but all agreements should contain certain elements. Two of these are: (a) a "high support" component; and (b) a program service arrangement component with a statement of goals, objectives, schedules, and routines that are associated with the delivery of services.

"High Support" Component

An agreement should not merely specify the services to be delivered or their objectives. Work with hard-to-employ job applicants requires that support be given to the applicant in the company work environment. To provide this support, it is usually necessary to negotiate an agreement to remove barriers to employment of the hard-to-employ, to modify the demands of the company's supervisory structure, and to give agency representatives (e.g., the job coach) prerogatives to advocate for their clients or to intervene in crises that may threaten the clients' continued employment.

An excellent model of a high support agreement is that developed in 1967-1968 by the JOBS NOW agency in Chicago. Job program developers required cooperating companies to institute high support provisions for placed participants such as:

1. lowering educational requirements
2. considering police records individually

3. lowering minimum standards on tests
4. assigning a co-worker as a "buddy"
5. consulting on the job (participant, JOBS NOW staff, and company supervisor)
6. making contact with JOBS NOW when employee's performance faltered
7. consulting with JOBS NOW before discharging participant
8. providing longer periods of orientation and training. [1]

The effectiveness of these high support agreements is attested to by the fact that the retention rate for companies that had instituted eight or more provisions was about three times greater than for companies that had instituted fewer than three provisions. [2]

Program Service Arrangements

A second major component of an agency-company agreement is the specification of services to be delivered. Such agreements require a detailed plan, beginning with the agency goals and operational objectives and moving to targets for service delivery and the schedules and routines that accompany these. The importance of this component of the agreement cannot be over-emphasized. It requires a commitment of resources from both the company and the agency.

Goals are abstract statements of ends on which agency and company personnel have agreed. They take the form of statements such as "to increase the receptivity of the company to minority-group employment" or "to build innovative manpower programs." The goals must be broken down into a set of concrete and realizable operational objectives, which are less abstract than goals and provide guidelines for actions, such as "to present a two-week orientation program for new employees." The operational objectives in turn must be converted into targets by assigning time dimensions to them. Thus, an operational objective becomes "to develop a 100-man capacity job counseling program by September 1, 1980." Finally, the targets must be specified in terms of routines and scheduled activities. The process can be outlined as in Figure 1.

A detailed and planned agreement has several advantages. First, the agency is able to arrange its priorities to combine operational staff and agency resources to serve a particular company. Staff workers can be assigned responsibilities with detailed work plans. Second, such an agreement can be used as a tool to evaluate the effectiveness of the agency operation in the company. By charting progress on each objective and observing work routines associated with that objective, the agency administrator can pinpoint the weak spots in a service program and identify further action required to accomplish the objective. The agreement plan thus can be used not only to compare what is and what should be happening in a given company but also to determine what procedures must be changed to make a given objective or target realizable in subsequent agency-company relationships.

Finally, the agreement plan is a device for reducing uncertainty. Participation in the agency-company relationship is frequently viewed by corporate staff in terms of costs and benefits to the company. What time commitments must the company make? What corporate personnel must be committed? What is to be gained from participation in the relationship with

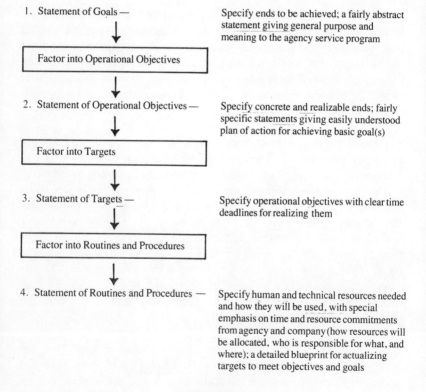

1. Statement of Goals — Specify ends to be achieved; a fairly abstract statement giving general purpose and meaning to the agency service program

Factor into Operational Objectives

2. Statement of Operational Objectives — Specify concrete and realizable ends; fairly specific statements giving easily understood plan of action for achieving basic goal(s)

Factor into Targets

3. Statement of Targets — Specify operational objectives with clear time deadlines for realizing them

Factor into Routines and Procedures

4. Statement of Routines and Procedures — Specify human and technical resources needed and how they will be used, with special emphasis on time and resource commitments from agency and company (how resources will be allocated, who is responsible for what, and where); a detailed blueprint for actualizing targets to meet objectives and goals

FIGURE 1
Service Planning Process

the agency? Unless these questions are answered, the agency-company relationship will be characterized by uncertainty. It must be realized that the question of company participation will be debated, analyzed, and decided upon by various groups of company personnel. Unless the plan has been factored in the terms stated above and committed to writing, it will be difficult for company personnel to grasp what the agency is trying to do, how it is going to do it, and what the costs and benefits to the company will be. Thus, the activity of communicating goals and objectives is of paramount importance in agency-company relationships and problems arise when a detailed statement of goals, objectives, targets, and routines is lacking.

THE ART OF NEGOTIATION

Good negotiators are made, not born. Bargaining and negotiation skills have to be acquired through in-service training (e.g., role playing simulation games) and practical experience. Some of the information about bargaining and negotiations that must be considered in planning training programs for agency personnel will be discussed here. This information is derived from a wide variety of sources: collective bargaining literature, international mediation concepts, and agency-company bargaining experiences. All of these sources contain general principles and concepts that can be applied to any bargaining situation, including the agency-company negotiation process. Particular care has been taken to specify the stages of bargaining, the strategies that are most useful, the agency resources that are needed, and the problems that are likely to occur.

It must be remembered that negotiation is a process in which verbal statements must be probed for hidden meanings. The best example of the hidden meaning statement is the assertion: "No, we do not want to do business with your agency." The skilled negotiator quickly recognizes that such a statement really means: "No, we do not want to do business with your agency under the conditions you have presented." "No" simply indicates that the issues and conditions of service must be re-examined to find a combination on which agreement is possible.

PREPARING FOR
NEGOTIATION SESSIONS

Most agency preparations for agency-company negotiations should begin with a period of probing and information gathering. This procedure involves identifying attitudes and positions of key company personnel, as well as structural features of the company, which will predispose it to accept certain agency services and refuse others.

Negotiating an agreement requires advance planning in which: (a) it is decided who will present the agency case and be its advocate in the bargaining; (b) alternative service plans are developed; (c) the agency's positions on certain issues are defined; and (d) provisions of the prospective agreement are specified. Without this preparation, the agency negotiator is under heavy pressure to make snap decisions with inadequate information. The end result can be an agreement that is not geared to the problems of corporate personnel and/or the service capacities of the agency.

Selecting the Person(s) to Represent the Agency in Negotiations

The choice of personnel to represent the agency should be related to the objectives of the negotiations, which usually are: (a) to obtain a policy commitment to take services; (b) to specify an acceptable service delivery package; and (c) to develop a written agreement with provisions for implementation of service delivery. Many agencies rely on a single individual to achieve all three objectives. In other cases, one individual is held responsible but he or she can call in other agency personnel when necessary. Other agencies make use of a negotiation team, carefully selecting individuals with differing expertise. The use of a single person poses problems, since it is rare that one individual has prestige in the agency, knows the program operations in sufficient detail, and has all of the technical and administrative skills necessary to accomplish all of these objectives.

In selecting members of a negotiation team, the following considerations are important:

1. A "top dog" of the agency, having sufficient authority and prestige to interact with a "top dog" counterpart in the company, should be included. The concern is with policy commitments from the company.

2. Staff who will be involved in administering the services (usually the heads of the appropriate service departments) should be included. The concern here is with the administrative feasibility of any plan that is developed.

3. Operational and technical personnel who will be delivering the services should be included. The concern here is with the technical feasibility of any agreement that is drawn up. An additional concern is the role of the

agency client group in the negotiation process. In a sense, clients are not represented: although service issues of great concern to clients are being debated, they are not at the bargaining meetings nor do they usually have mechanisms for expressing their views. Although the agency personnel represent the clients' interests, agency negotiators may not know the clients well. Care should be taken to involve agency personnel who work directly with clients and are sensitive to their needs.

Not all of these members need to be included in every meeting, but their combined input should be reflected in any negotiated agreement. A sound practice is to involve as many of them as possible in planning the negotiations in order to obtain their guidance on possible problems, specific language, and terms of the working agreement.

Since the agency's case may be presented poorly if there are a number of speakers contradicting each other, the selection of a spokesman is a basic consideration. The characteristics of an ideal spokesman are:

1. The person should be articulate, persuasive, and patient. He or she should be able to restate agency proposals in simple terms beginning with the phrase: "Our objective is . . . ."

2. The person should have a detailed knowledge of agency practices, rules, and regulations and a realistic picture of the agency's capabilities and competencies.

3. The person should have a knowledge of general corporate practices and the specific practices of the company with which the agency is dealing.

4. The person should enjoy negotiating and bargaining. He or she should have an understanding of the negotiation process and be able to work under pressure. The person does not have to like his or her company counterparts but should be able to understand their positions and the conditions that sustain these.

If the agency has no one who is experienced in negotiations, it is probably wise to designate as spokesman someone who is widely respected within the agency and has a reputation for fairness. In speaking for the agency, he or she must be able to relate to a broad range of agency personnel, understand their positions on issues to be negotiated, and be trusted by them not to compromise recklessly on their preferences.

Developing Alternative Service Plans

Rarely will a company buy a comprehensive package of services all at once. Usually the company will accept a single service or a limited package of services, which later may be renewed or expanded. Since there is no way to predict management needs, it is sound practice to formulate a number of service plan alternatives beforehand. One alternative may be to do less than desired with fewer people than necessary in order to demonstrate the advisability of broadening the scope of services. Another alternative may be to deliver a service (e.g., counseling) without the usual supportive services. Several points should be noted in developing these alternatives:

1. The alternatives should be real choices and not merely the same plan labeled in several different ways.

2. Steps should be taken to anticipate and specify the strategy that is most appropriate in presenting each plan.

3. Appropriate and frequent consultation with the agency's operational personnel should accompany the development of each plan. This consultation not only provides a test of the feasibility of each plan but also builds a commitment to the alternative service packages. It precludes the possibility of intra-agency conflict resulting from divided opinion on the efficacy of the various plans.

4. Some preliminary exploration of company attitudes and positions may be desirable to determine the range of plans that would be acceptable. It is often possible to obtain some indication by discussing the plans informally with members of the company's personnel and technical departments. These plans should be based on the realities of the company's operation.

Determining the Agency's Positions on Issues

The agency bargaining team must not plan for negotiations under the principle of "all or nothing" but must determine beforehand the profile of an "acceptable deal." This does not mean that all parts of the service package must be negotiated away or that the team must be committed to one deal. Advance planning is necessary to establish enough flexibility to accomplish the objective of negotiation and bargaining, which is to obtain an agreement.

Guidelines to determining agency positions, particularly on issues requiring flexibility, are:

1. Recognize the necessity of involving as many agency operational personnel as possible in order to obtain their guidance on problems and on terms to be used in negotiating and implementing an agreement. These staff members are familiar with operational problems. In addition, since they will administer the agreement, they must be involved in structuring it.

2. Review the problems that have occurred in past agency-company relationships, particularly the issues that led to disputes between agency and company personnel. If the number and mode of contact situations have been a recurrent problem, the agency negotiator can maintain a position on this issue designed to avoid such disputes. An adequate review should not be confined to trouble areas but should also identify positions and relationships that have worked out well in the past.

3. Review and analyze the target company's history of doing business with agencies. Interviews with officials of these agencies frequently reveal what the company has been expecting elsewhere and what issues give the most trouble. This information will enable the negotiator to formulate a range of expectations about the company personnel.

4. Solicit from the company a statement of its plans in the area to be discussed. What objectives does the company have and what targets are under consideration? Agency positions should fit within the framework of these plans.

Spelling Out Provisions and Wording the Agreement

In the pre-negotiation stages, the agency negotiation team must consider not only the content of the agreement but also its wording. These are not by-products of the negotiations but in most cases are inputs into the negotiation process. Since the language of the agreement determines how it will be administered, it must be planned in considerable detail in advance of the negotiations:

1. The specific language of the proposed agreement should be thoroughly planned. If the negotiator has a number of positions or provisions, he or she must be prepared with alternative language forms. The negotiator should be ready to explain in simple terms what the alternatives are and should avoid technical language and jargon.

2. Particularly after the first agreement, an appropriate tool is a "bargaining book," with present language on the left and desired alternatives on the right.

3. To ensure that the agreement will work in practice, the administrators and operational personnel should be consulted before and after the proposed language is drafted.

4. Alternative language should be considered in advance. There are many different ways to word objectives. At all costs, ambiguous or value-laden words (e.g., "evaluation" for "retrieval of information") should be avoided.

5. Company questions and agency responses to them should be anticipated. If the negotiator has prepared well and knows the target company and its problems, he should receive no surprises.

6. In every meeting, there are two agendas: (a) the company's proposals and (b) what is behind them. The agency should examine every proposal and try to identify the conditions within the company that have led to its formulation.

THE CONDUCT OF NEGOTIATIONS

The conduct of negotiations is ready to begin when: (a) the negotiating team has been selected; (b) the spokesman for the team has been selected; and (c) the proposals have been prepared (with adequate provision for minimum, intermediate, and maximum positions).

There are a number of procedural points that can influence the climate in which negotiations occur:

1. *Keeping a record*. Tape recording the sessions should be done only with the consent of both agency and company personnel and should not be a substitute for recordkeeping. Recordkeeping ideally should be a shared activity in which one member of each party keeps notes, the notes are compared, and an attempt is made to secure agreement by both parties that the notes represent an objective record of the meeting. A system of "session minutes" prepared jointly is usually sufficient and should be distributed shortly after each meeting.

2. *Place of meeting*. It should be reasonably isolated and comfortable and should have a convenient "break-up" or caucus room. Advance arrangements should be made for a blackboard or other required props.

STEPS IN NEGOTIATION

Without pre-planning, negotiations can be open-ended. At some point, critical decisions must be made: what is the target date for an agreement? how many meetings should be held? what amount of time should be committed to working out an agreement? Although arbitrary target dates should be avoided, necessity frequently imposes them. The company may need the service during a specific time period. The agency has other priorities, and time spent with this company must be balanced against other commitments. The negotiation process should be viewed as a series of linked problem-solving meetings, and the obvious answer to the question of a target date is that sufficient time must be spent exploring mutual concerns, developing operational objectives, defusing and resolving disputes, and working out an agreement.

These activities usually proceed through four steps: (a) establishing the negotiation range; (b) reconnoitering the range of issues; (c) narrowing the range of concerns; and (d) writing the agreement.

Establishing the Negotiation Range

This step beings with "getting to know each other" and considerable time may be spent on topics unrelated to the service capabilities of the agency. Frequently what is involved is an attempt by members of the agency and company teams to establish a personal image as well as to size up the members of the opposite team.

A second phase of this step involves attempts by company members to learn more about the agency, its objectives, and its capabilities. On the agency side, there is a desire to know more about the company, its problems, and its perspectives on the kind of service being offered. There are often several meetings during this stage.

Several points should be noted here:

1. This step will be characterized by uncertainty, shifting ground, and indecisiveness. It lacks a clear goal orientation but is essential before moving on to more focused discussion.

111

2. Usually each member of both teams should be given a chance to create an identity. However, team members should make it clear that their remarks are enlargements of the spokesman's position rather than opposing views.

3. There will be many questions posed by company personnel in this step, and how they are answered can determine the course of negotiations. Questions should not be avoided. The fact that service programs frequently require time and manpower commitments from the company cannot be disguised, but estimates of the amount of time and the number of personnel can be set aside for the future.

4. In all parts of the negotiations, but particularly in this step, the participants should listen carefully.

5. Participants should be careful of empathic conversational gambits which can hurt by increasing the other side's expectations.

6. The negotiator should give himself time to think. One effective strategy is to give the ball to someone else on his team.

7. The negotiator should not avoid issues by hiding behind the phrase "agency policy." He should be able to explain why the agency holds a particular position.

Reconnoitering the Range of Issues

The second step in negotiation is focused on concrete problem solving. There is less concern with establishing identities and more concern with probing for commitments to courses of action proposed by agency personnel. To narrow the range of issues, the agency negotiator talks in terms of possibilities, not certainties. Tentative agreements occur in this step and should be recorded. These tentative agreements can easily be lost and agency and company personnel frequently have to negotiate an issue twice.

1. In order to record some successes at the beginning and build up a momentum, the negotiator should start with easy issues. Starting with complicated or troublesome issues creates a climate of hostility that could flavor subsequent steps of the negotiations. These issues should be put aside but not forgotten.

2. One plan or service should not be oversold. Rigid early agreements on service delivery may be difficult to change if the agency has engaged in a "hard sell."

3. The agency negotiator should know the capacities, capabilities, and resources of the agency and should limit exploration to services he knows can be delivered. If the service requested by company personnel is beyond the agency's resources, this fact should be frankly acknowledged. Agency personnel frequently are plied with service requests beyond the agency's capabilities, but fear that admission of the agency's limitations will damage the presentation of their case to company personnel.

Narrowing the Range of Concerns

The third step in negotiation brings the features of the agreement into sharp focus. The concern here is with bridging the last gap between discussion and agreement. This step inevitably involves a decision-reaching crisis. Timing and pacing are the important considerations. Should company personnel be pushed to make a commitment or should they be left to make the decision at their own speed? Pushing for an immediate decision entails the risk of producing an agreement to which the company management feels no commitment. Leaving the situation open-ended may result in the failure of company personnel to commit themselves at all. The choice is a difficult one, but the problem must be faced.

1. Normally, circumstances will dictate a deadline for reaching the point at which company personnel must make a decision. Scheduling work within the agency's and the company's expectations of a date for beginning services usually will impose a deadline toward which the negotiations must proceed. Since the agency must arrange its working priorities to service a number of companies, the agency negotiator may have to create an artificial deadline by designating a date by which discussions must conclude. It should be recognized, however, that in many cases protracted negotiation will be necessary and that patience is essential. Experience and training of the agency negotiators can give them the skills and strategies to terminate negotiations and move on to agreement and commitment.

2. It is a good rule not to propose a final agreement until the negotiator is certain that all major issues have been discussed and all information is available to both parties.

3. Since the chances of agreement are slim if only one option is presented, alternatives should be proposed and the range of possible solutions to problems increased. The alternatives should be phrased not in terms of ''yes'' and ''no'' but rather in terms of ''plan A'' and ''plan B.''

4. It should be recognized that at all steps of the negotiations company personnel must check with their superior, particularly in the last steps, where company commitments have to be made. The negotiator should try to ascertain how much decision-making authority and flexibility company personnel have and in what form their presentation to their superior will be made. Agency personnel should explore the possibility of joining in that presentation to avoid misinterpretation or to answer further questions. It would be a mistake to believe that agreement with company personnel at a meeting means company agreement. In almost all cases, the agreement is not an agreement until it is reviewed, discussed, and approved by top management officials.

Writing the Agreement

The main requirement in writing the agreement is that its language be unambiguous and understood by both parties. Jargon and technical terms can cause considerable misunderstanding. The length of the written agreement is secondary in importance to the clarity of the ideas, objectives, and scheduled routines associated with the services.

Two major issues should be noted in the writing of an agreement:

1. The agreement should be written as the negotiations progress and not as a final action. As agreements are reached, they should be recorded and their wording approved by both parties. The final written agreement is a cumulation of these sub-agreements. If the writing of the agreement is conceived as an act separate from negotiations, it may be necessary to renegotiate issues. Each sub-agreement should be approved as the negotiations proceed and a record of the approval distributed to both parties.

2. Many sub-agreements are reached informally or in non-negotiation situations. Converting these informal agreements to written ones is a major problem because they are rarely recorded on the spot and there may be no witnesses to substantiate them. Although a basic rule is to record everything that occurs, even in informal contact, the informal contact situation frequently precludes a strong sense of agreement.

TECHNIQUES FOR RESOLVING
BARGAINING IMPASSES

The essence of negotiation skill is the ability to remain problem-oriented. It must be recognized, however, that despite this orientation some impasses will develop and that strategies must be learned to resolve them:

1. An issue that has reached an impasse should be set aside and other issues considered. This strategy creates an image of movement and provides momentum that would not be possible if attention remained focused on one issue.

2. Frequently, an issue may be removed from an impasse by assigning it to a special "study group" composed of representatives of both parties. This strategy usually works with technical problems but is less useful with general issues. Thus, a subcommittee may resolve an impasse over the form of a reporting system but rarely will settle an issue such as whether an agency follow-up program should be developed.

3. In some cases, an impasse may be broken by an off-the-record conference. By mutual agreement, no notes are to be taken and the matters discussed are not to be made public. Speaking off the record, company personnel frequently will divulge inside information that can provide in-sights into ways of resolving the impasse.

THE ADMINISTRATION
OF THE AGREEMENT

The written agreement between the company and the agency is useful only insofar as it is widely diffused and understood by the personnel in both agencies. A standard practice of agency personnel should be to attempt to follow up the agreement by becoming involved in the diffusion process in the company. Several strategies can be used to accomplish this objective:

1. If company management can be persuaded to agree, small group meetings of company personnel at all levels (particularly those involved in the working of the agreement) should be held to discuss and analyze the agreement as well as to answer questions. Every attempt should be made to personalize the agreement by defining each individual's role in it. Wherever possible, agency personnel should be present to provide information and to answer questions. In many companies, particularly those with rigid supervisory structures, the initiation of such meetings is difficult.

2. Knowledge of the agreement, its goals, and its objectives should be built into company supervisory training programs. This strategy provides wide diffusion of the agreement and the provisions of the agreement serve as inputs to company in-service training programs.

3. Poor administration can undermine what was originally a good agreement. Once the agreement is signed, agency personnel cannot rest on their laurels; they must set up the machinery both to implement the agreement and to ensure that it is working. The agreement can easily be eroded through lack of follow-up. Periodic meetings involving both company and agency personnel, particularly those who are involved in implementation, are necessary to review the agreement. Bargaining, agreement, and follow-up must be seen as parts of a single process contributing to the maintenance of the agency-company relationship.

FOOTNOTES

1. David Rogers, *JOBS NOW Project, Final Report for Phase One*, JOBS NOW Project (Chicago: U.S. Department of Labor Contract No. 82015068-08, 1968).

2. Ibid.

MANAGEMENT BY OBJECTIVES:
A GOALS PROGRAM FOR
DIVERSE ORGANIZATIONS

Neil F. Shiffler

Many good managers have found that when they have a direction in which to focus their efforts, accomplishment and satisfaction follow. While this concept is not new, in the past five or ten years it has frequently been formalized by corporations and individual managers and given such names as ''management by objectives'' and ''goal setting.'' These have common objectives and their basic methods are the same. Many managers are now using some of these methods in their everyday activities and in planning for the future.

The ''goals'' method is not a technique or an addition to the manager's job, but a way of managing. It is a commitment approach that compels the manager to continually strive to improve his organization's performance and to further his own self-development. In order to survive, organizations must improve every year: improvement must be a way of life. The ''goals'' method should result in a better understanding of, involvement in, and commitment to corporate and sub-division goals as well as fulfillment of individual goals such as growth, achievement, and recognition, which provide optimum satisfaction and motivation.

SEMANTICS

One of the initial obstacles to explaining and understanding the ''goals'' concept is in the meaning of terms. The following definitions make explicit both the relationships and the differences among various management terms.

Objectives. ''Objectives'' is the term normally used to describe targets set at the corporate and departmental levels. They are the fundamental base for the lower-level goals. They may range in time span from one to five years.

Goals. Goals are targets set at levels other than corporate and departmental levels. They include: (1) goals wholly under the control of the manager and/or his own subordinates; (2) goals related to higher levels of the

117

organization, in the setting of which the manager can play a partial role; and (3) goals related to other levels of the organization, either higher or lower.

The goal process may be regarded as a "management improvement process." The goalsetter asks: "What are our normal, regular, on-going responsibilities? What can we do to improve our management processes?" Thus, while related to normal operations, goals identify those specific areas or programs in which change and improvement are needed and possible. Goal statements can and should be concise. They tell what is to be achieved and when it is to be achieved.

Work Plans. Work plans spell out how the goals will be reached. They need not be very detailed but should be seen as a facilitating or implementing tool for reaching the goals set. They also provide the base for progress reviews.

Work Plan Progress Reviews. Work plan progress reviews are discussions between the manager and his subordinate, aimed specifically at reviewing progress on goals and related work plans. Their major purpose is to determine whether progress is being made and, if it is not, what steps are needed to achieve it. These reviews may take place within whatever time span is appropriate — weekly, monthly, quarterly, or annually. They should be as informal as possible and should encourage mutual problem solving rather than control and direction by the manager.

Performance Review. A performance review is normally conducted annually, although it may be conducted more frequently if desired. Its purpose is to review not only the goals program but also the overall work performance of an individual. While the review will, of course, be related to regular performance and to the goals program, it should also form the basis for discussion of employee career goals, training, and development and changes in the system or work situation needed to help improve performance.

Salary Review. The annual salary review is an evaluation of the employee's overall performance, as well as his performance on his specific goals. However, while clearly related to these two key areas, the salary review obviously involves other factors as well. The checklist in Appendix I shows all the factors normally involved in salary review decisions. Understanding of this (by both the supervisor and his subordinates) is an essential starting point.

BASIC CONCEPTS

The concept of goal-setting or managing by objectives, as it is practiced today, is based on recent research findings of behavioral scientists, especially in the areas of motivation and commitment. While most of the ideas are not new, there are several important aspects that must be clearly understood if the concept is to be successfully utilized.

To start with, when a manager has a clear understanding of his responsibilities, he has a head start on achieving meaningful results. Often individuals are frustrated in their total effort to do a good job because their picture of what they are to accomplish is hazy. Position descriptions and bits of information from the boss or from their peers are not sufficient. If intense focus on results is lacking, individuals may engage in many "busy" or "comfortable" activities. With this climate prevailing, most individuals have little or no motivation; their growth and the organization's growth suffer. To say this in a positive way: when a person has to think of his work in terms of the results he will produce, it becomes easier to separate the necessary activities from the merely desirable and to separate both from the irrelevant.

Secondly, it is mandatory for the individual to have an appreciable influence in setting his own goals if he is to be committed to achieving them. Of course he cannot set his goals with little regard for the organization's requirements or without his boss's agreement that the goals are desirable. The heart of the MBO concept is that individual needs and goals must be integrated with organizational goals and must be achieved concurrently. The process by which the goals are set and the nature of the goals themselves affect the ability of an individual to meet this dual responsibility. The basic question is not whether the goals should be set by the subordinate or the manager, but what each should contribute to setting them. As with many other aspects of managing, manipulation, forced acceptance, lack of sincerity, or pressure for compliance in the process lays open the possibility for undesirable consequences, such as antagonism toward the supervisor, noncompliance, unreliable performance, the need for close surveillance, and high administrative costs. The concept of management by objectives must be built from a climate of trust between the employee and his supervisor, in which the employee is in a contest situation between himself and his goals and the supervisor acts as coach, with the responsibility of giving assistance and support.

It is obvious that attaining the optimum mixture of freedom and of supervisor or organization influence is critical. While we are not industrial psychologists who can thoroughly understand the drives of each individual, common sense and experience have taught us that each employee must be handled differently. For this reason, it is important that the supervisor be aware of differences and that the goal setting be done not on a team basis but in a one-to-one discussion situation. When a section or department becomes proficient in using goals, team review and coordination of individuals' goals are both desirable and helpful.

The third basic aspect is in the goals themselves. They must be goals that require "stretch" and do not merely forecast what probably will happen. On the other hand, they cannot be unrealistic for the individual's capabilities or for the external factors prevailing. They must be end results, be very specific, be measurable if possible, and have a specified time for completion. They are results which are important to the success of the business and which may require innovation and creativity. A needed break-through in a crucial area is an appropriate focus for a goal. Goal accomplishment must help the individual and the organization progress toward attainment of long-range goals.

Fourth — and probably the aspect of goal-setting we do least well at present — is the requirement for progress review. It is not enough to put well-meaning and well-defined goals on paper at the beginning of the year and then not look at them until the year has run its course. An annual review of accomplishment is better than no review at all, but still almost ineffective. Once goals are set and agreed to by the employee and his supervisor, a definite cycle of oral progress reviews between the two is necessary. The time interval will depend on significant data available and kinds of goals set. The maximum time between reviews is three months and the minimum as little as one or two weeks, as in cases where only a few short-term goals have been set. The shorter interval is especially appropriate for the lower levels of supervision.

GOALS PROGRAMS FOR HUMAN SERVICE ORGANIZATIONS

Table 1 shows organizational and MBO comparisons for industry and human services. Most social agencies are classified as dynamic organizations — that is, they operate in an environment that is constantly changing or where there is more uncertainty than in a bureaucratic organization.

In a dynamic organization, persons perform a greater variety of tasks that are nonprogrammed and nonrepetitive. Members of such an organization frequently work in project groups or work teams, mixing with different supervisors and organization members. A major problem with measuring effectiveness in some human service organizations is that there is disagreement among the various interest groups as to what the priorities are or should be. Different groups have different goals, and these goals change. Therefore, when implementing a goals program, it is useful to think of these organizations as having a negotiated order.

TABLE 1
Organizational and MBO Comparisons

Organizational Comparisons

Industrial	Human Service
1. Hierarchical structure with policies, plans, and procedures used to resolve conflict in objectives and overcome restraints	A charismatic leader and/or the "mystique" of the organization used to resolve conflict in objectives and overcome restraints
2. Bureaucratic (more stable) organization	Dynamic organization
3. More diversified employee allegiance, i.e., company, work group, social group, self, etc.	More worker commitment to professions or mission
4. Clear, overriding enterprise objectives	Mission statements (often ambiguous) and goals
5. Uses rewards and punishments for goal attainment	Rewards more related to length of service and experience

MBO Comparisons

Industrial	Human Service
1. Emphasis on end results	Some emphasis on end results, more emphasis on action plans
2. Emphasis on "hard" criteria	More emphasis on "soft" criteria
3. Economic outcomes	More noneconomic outcomes stressed (intangible, hard to measure)
4. Deductive process for action plans (basically top-down)	Inductive process for action plans (basically bottom-up)
5. Used as efficiency and effectiveness measurement	Best used for planning and communication

MBO as used in business and industry frequently is modified to meet the needs of human service organizations. As "hard" criteria are more difficult to obtain in a dynamic organization than in a stable organization, MBO must usually be undertaken on a different basis. "Hard" criteria are viewed as ends or levels and indicate nothing about attaining these ends or levels. On the contrary, "soft" criteria show that an event has or has not occurred and do not indicate a level of achievement.

In MBO for human service organizations, the definition of activities for goal achievement should be emphasized. A general objective is stated and an action plan given in detail, with the person or group evaluated on the basis of whether the action plan is being followed. It is assumed that if the plan is followed, the goal will eventually be reached. In effect, this strategy attempts to ensure that organization members go through the steps that are assumed to lead toward the goal. Where possible, "soft" criteria might be supported with other data to minimize substantial distortions of behavior.

In summary, human service organizations can apply the industrial MBO approach to their operations with minimal modification. Although judgment about good or poor performance is necessarily subjective and although private donors or the government often impose special conditions for continuing support, the realities of today's environment necessitate the application of some management techniques to the operations of social agencies.

Most organizations, particularly larger ones with multiple managerial levels, currently use some "end results" measurement (formal or informal) as a part of their planning and control. However, they find the extension of a goals program to other organizational areas more difficult and/or they meet resistance. An MBO plan for adapting and/or extending a goals program for many human service organizations can be achieved by:

1. establishing mission statements and major organizational goals
2. establishing goals and action plans, following the inductive (bottom-up) approach
3. emphasizing "soft" criteria, using professional standards where possible
4. focusing measurement on the action plan (or the activities), with "milestones" used to approximate progress and
5. initially emphasizing the "goals" approach primarily for planning and communication purposes rather than for measuring effectiveness.

MECHANICS

The mechanics of a goals program can be approached in several ways; to arbitrarily impose a single procedure would be inconsistent with the basic philosophy of the program itself. However, there are five basic steps which are essential to the successful implementation and operation of such a program:

1. Agreement must be reached between the individual and his superior on the areas in which results are expected and on the means of determining accomplishment in these areas.

2. The individual must be given appreciable influence in determining the goals if he is to be committed to their attainment.

3. Feedback of performance information must be given to the individual as data become available. This procedure allows the individual to see where he stands on each of his goals and to take any necessary corrective action.

4. At several interim points in the goals accomplishment period the individual must report orally to his superior on his progress toward accomplishment of the goals and discuss any changes, modifications, or problems. The superior acts as a coach in this situation, providing advice and offering suggestions, if needed, to assist in accomplishment of the goals.

5. At the end of the goals accomplishment period, the individual must prepare a written goals accomplishment report and review it with his superior. The emphasis in the accomplishment review is on learning. As in the progress review, the superior acts as a coach and the discussion centers around building on successful accomplishment and finding ways to improve in areas in which the individual has not been successful.

The ''Goals Program Model'' shown in Figure 1 illustrates these essential steps within the framework of a total goals accomplishment period. Two significant aspects of the model should be pointed out:

1. The responsibility for initiating discussions on results areas and goals as well as progress and accomplishment reviews is placed on the subordinate.

2. No time period is specified for the cycle from goal setting to the target date for accomplishment. Depending upon the nature of the job and the goals set, this accomplishment period can be of any length up to a year. However, it is important that the progress reviews be held at regular intervals within the cycle. These intervals should not exceed three months when an annual cycle is used, as experience shows the motivational value of the scheduled follow-up tends to lessen after this period of time.

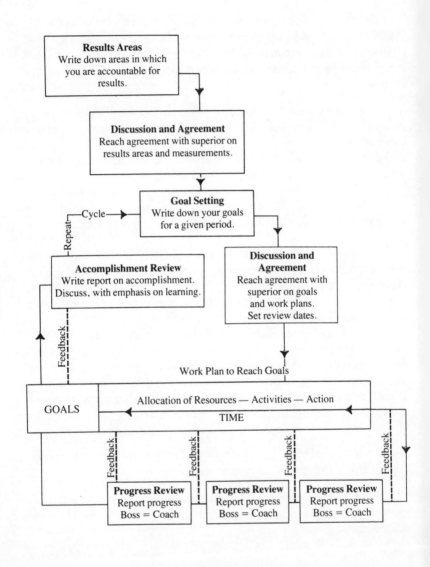

FIGURE 1
Goals Program Model

124

DISCUSSION AND CONCLUSIONS

In a hasty and sometimes haphazard approach to MBO, a manager may be unable to avoid pitfalls because he is unaware of them. Some of these pitfalls are as follows:

1. The manager does not focus on the individual subordinate as the prime factor in the success or failure of MBO, but instead concentrates on the procedures, the forms, and the overall approaches to MBO. In fact, the manager's ability to convey the notion of MBO, to train and develop his subordinates, and to focus his attention on the individual may be the critical factors in the successful use of MBO.

2. The way in which the concept is presented to subordinates frequently makes it appear to be an additional responsibility rather than a way for the individual to manage his own activities. Viewing MBO as added work, subordinates may have negative attitudes toward the accomplishment of someone else's goals.

3. Managers often overlook the fact that MBO requires a new style of management. A high degree of concentration on one's own leadership style may be necessary if some of the old authoritarian ways are to be given up and new, more participative ways established. MBO is not something to be done occasionally but must be monitored on a day-to-day basis.

4. A manager may believe that MBO can be installed in a short span of time. On the average, a manager can spend a year and a half to two years learning to manage by objectives and subordinates may require an equal amount of time to learn how to use MBO. When departmental, divisional, or higher levels in the organization are considered, the length of time is extended and, in some cases, as long as eight to ten years may be required to make the system operable throughout the organization.

5. Sometimes managers insist that their subordinates change but they themselves do not change. The discrepancy between what a manager says he wants his subordinates to do and what he himself is doing creates conflict.

6. Managers frequently lack the skills (including listening, questioning, and diagnostic skills) necessary to make MBO work effectively. A manager who has avoided the previous pitfalls may fail because he does not have the skills to communicate to his subordinates how the system works.

The success of MBO depends on four factors. First, a manager's basic beliefs about how subordinates function or should function in an organization affect his ability to use MBO. If a manager believes that people need to be told how they should function, MBO probably will not work. If he believes that his subordinates have the ability and willingness to accept the responsibility for and control of their own activities and results, MBO probably will work.

Second, a manager must be willing to learn the basic concept of MBO and understand its behavioral implications. He must develop a clear understanding of how people are motivated.

Third, while reshaping attitudes and learning about the basic concepts of MBO, a manager should be developing his listening, communication, questioning, and diagnostic skills.

Fourth, a successful MBO approach involves a systematic understanding of how it works and a step-by-step development of the program, starting usually with the development of the manager's own ability to manage by objectives and extending, individual by individual or unit by unit, throughout his organization. MBO will work only if the manager takes the approach of carefully designing, implementing, testing, and diagnosing to ensure that the basic steps are followed. It requires an openness, a willingness to trust others in the organization, and a sharing of responsibility.

The essence of MBO is that it allows the individual to function as a whole person within the context of the organization.

APPENDIX I
Goal Planning Worksheet

Specific Goal to be Achieved	Goal Attainment Criteria	Goal Schedule	Begin	Complete	Progress Review and Evaluation
To develop "Supermarket" concept of compensation within limits of approved payroll budget for Third Line Managers by (date).	Specific evidence regarding new policies and adopted and implemented by ten percent of Third Line Managers by (date).	1. Research concept and experience of other companies.			
		2. Make preliminary determination regarding which programs are adaptable to concept.			
		3. Consider additional programs, if any, that should be developed for X Company.			
		4. Consult with Legal and Financial Departments to determine legality and tax status of various alternative "packages."			
		5. Develop proposed "package" arrangements and consult with Financial Department about mechanics of pricing alternatives.			
		6. Consult with Employee Relations Department about benefit plan changes contemplated for Union Personnel to ensure that arrangements are sufficiently flexible to fit concept. If not, consider alternative approaches required for Managers.			
		7. Draft proposal regarding concept for top Management review and approval or comment.			
		8. Upon approval, develop final details of program and communicate its existence to Third Line Managers.			
		9. Follow-up implementation of program; act as liaison with Financial Department.			
		10. Evaluate program effectiveness and determine feasibility of extending to all Managers.			

APPENDIX II
Performance Review and Summary

(Recommended for use where the employee and his supervisor have mutually agreed on work plans and goals as a guide to the employee's performance over the appraisal period.)

Employee No.	Name (Last)	(First)	(Middle Initial)	Date of Birth

Position Code No.	Position Title	Salary Grade

Department	Division

Section	Location

From   To
Appraisal Period   Anniversary Date

A. Description of work plans and goals for this appraisal period.

1. The following items represent the major goals of this employee during this appraisal period.

_____

_____

_____

_____

B. Evaluation of employee's specific work accomplishments during the appraisal period.

1. The following items represent the employee's major work accomplishments during this period. These include (a) goals described in Section A which were accomplished as planned; and (b) major items accomplished which were not included in the goals developed for this period.

_____

_____

_____

_____

2. Analyze the value of these accomplishments relative to the responsibilities of the employee's position and of the work group as a whole. Consider quality, quantity, timeliness, and relative importance and impact of the work performed.

_____

_____

_____

_____

3. The following major items were not accomplished as planned.

_____

_____

_____

_____

4. The following factors which existed during this period made it easier or more difficult for this employee to achieve these results.

_____

_____

_____

_____

_____

C. Overall conclusion of performance level and trend during the appraisal period.

1. Level of performance:
   ____ Outstanding   ____ Marginal   ____ Acceptable
   ____ Fully Competent   ____ Superior   ____ Unsatisfactory
2. Trend of performance
   ____ Improving   ____ Static   ____ Declining

Appraisal By: _____
                    Name   Title   Date

Reviewed By: _____
                    Name   Title   Date

Remarks: _____

_____

_____

_____

APPENDIX III
Criteria for Identifying Results Areas

Industry	Human Service
1. Results areas should be titles suggesting results, not activities (i.e., nouns not verbs).	1. Results areas often are titles suggesting activities (often verbs), though focus should be on results if possible.
2. Adjectives denoting the desired quality should be avoided.	2. Adjectives denoting the desired quality should be avoided.
3. Results areas should not be combined (e.g., not "Production Planning," "Production Quality," etc.).	3. Results areas should not be combined (e.g., not "Health Services" but "Education & Research," "Home Care," "Rehabilitation Services," etc.).
4. The list should be as complete as possible and should indicate which responsibilities are the most important and which will take the most time.	4. The list should be as complete as possible and should indicate which responsibilities are the most important and which will take the most time.

APPENDIX IV
Criteria for Establishing Goals

Industry	Human Service
1. Stated in terms of end results	1. More likely stated in terms of activities
2. Achievable in definite period of time	2. More flexibility on time period
3. Definite form of accomplishment	3. Less definite and more subjective
4. Related to the management of the organization	4. Related to the management of the organization
5. In accord with department and company goals	5. In accord with mission statement and organizational objectives
6. Precisely stated in quantitative terms if possible	6. Progress toward goals estimated by reference to selected intermediate outcomes (milestones), stated in quantitative terms if possible
7. Limited to one important goal per statement	7. Limited to one important goal per statement
8. Require stretch	8. Require stretch

APPENDIX V
Some Quantitative and Qualitative Goals

Quantitative

Industry	Human Service
1. Complete construction of approved building within cost of $20,000.	1. Complete construction of approved building within cost of $20,000.
2. Reduce waiting period of customers' orders from two weeks to one week.	2. Reduce waiting period for counseling from two weeks to one week.
3. Maintain training and development costs at 1977 level.	3. Maintain training and development costs at 1977 level.
4. Establish a new distribution system in Sacramento by 1979.	4. Establish a new rehabilitation program in Sacramento by 1979.
5. Increase the dollar level of sales of ABC product by twenty percent in 1978.	5. Increase the number of referrals by twenty percent in 1978.

Qualitative

Industry	Human Service
1. Conduct monthly development sessions for plant superintendents in the techniques of standard cost program.	1. Conduct monthly development sessions for counselors in the techniques of dignosis and treatment of drug addiction.
2. Implement a program for counseling the ''soon to be retired.''	2. Implement a program for counseling alcoholics and their families.
3. Improve the quality of ABC product.	3. Improve the quality of patient care.
4. Establish a comprehensive career counseling program for the disadvantaged in the community.	4. Establish a comprehensive care system for the disadvantaged in the community.
5. Develop a review system for financial solvency and institutional survival.	5. Develop a review system for financial solvency and institutional survival.

REFERENCES

Guerin, Quentin W. "Management by Objectives and Assessment by Results." *Industrial Supervisors* (April 1971): 8-9.

Hughes, Charles L. *Goal Setting: Key to Individual and Organizational Effectiveness*. New York: American Management Association, 1965.

Humble, John W. *Management by Objectives in Action*. New York: McGraw-Hill, 1970.

Mahler, Walter R. "A Systems Approach to Managing by Objectives." *Systems and Procedures Journal* (September-October 1965): 12-19.

Newman, W. E., and Warren, E. K. *The Process of Management*. Englewood Cliffs, N.J.: Prentice-Hall, 1978.

Raider, Merlyn C. "Social Service Model." *Journal of Social Casework* (October 1976): 523-28.

Varney, Glenn H. "Management by Objectives: Making It Work." *Supervisory Management* (January 1972): 16-20.

MATCHING TREATMENT AND MANAGEMENT SYSTEMS IN CORRECTIONAL INSTITUTIONS

Richard Babcock
Peter F. Sorensen, Jr.

In two similar state youth correction institutions in the same state system, comparable operating results were achieved by using contrasting management systems: one participative and decentralized and other non-participative and centralized. The populations in these institutions were delinquent teen-age males. The purpose of this paper is to explain the theory base we developed and used in working as consultants with these institutions over a 2½ year period.

The institutions were a matched pair in terms of budgets, numbers of professional and managerial personnel, and populations. At the end of the 2½ year period, they were rated by internal evaluations of the Department of Corrections as superior institutions in the state system. The evaluations were based on the following major factors: the percentage of delinquents granted parole out of the total prison population, the recidivism rate (percentage of adolescents rearrested out of the total paroled after a three-month period), cost per adolescent (with a subjective weighting largely based on the age of the facility), and other subjective factors.

NEED FOR A THEORETICAL MODEL

In business management there is beginning to emerge a contingency theory, in which different management systems (to summarize, organic and mechanistic) are associated with different technologies and rates of change. While we were not aware of such a theory in the area of corrections, attempting to impose a single system of management on these institutions did not make sense.

By adopting the contingency theory, we developed a crude contingency model for these correctional institutions, with the contingency factor in the typology being the treatment systems. Treatment became analogous to technology and we hypothesized that the management system should be matched with the treatment system.

THE TREATMENT SYSTEMS

A brief description of the treatment systems follows to show how the environments in which we were working differed.

Site A

Positive peer culture involved developing ongoing juvenile groups or teams, which were matched with a team of professionals. The team of professionals developed a treatment program for each juvenile, guided him through an individualized program of rehabilitation in the peer group setting, and made parole recommendations and presentations.

Site B

Modified behavior modification was based on giving the juvenile population positive feedback and support. The ideal was to treat all juveniles consistently — i.e. to reward identified behaviors with positive feedback and support.

DEVELOPMENT OF THE THEORY

Figure 1 summarizes the theory we developed for the different sites. We felt that a participative treatment system should be matched with a participative management system, and vice versa. The personal orientations of top level managers (in particular the superintendents) had to be consistent with the technology (treatment part) of the theory.

Name of Institution	Treatment Philosophy and System	Management System
SITE A	Positive peer culture	Decentralized Group decision-making emphasis Overlapping line and team structure Group and individual objectives
SITE B	Positive feedback and support (modified behavior modification)	Centralized Formalized upward communication Predominantly line structure Emphasis on individual objectives

FIGURE 1
Treatment and Management Systems
At the Two Institutions

Site A

The prescription for Site A was to move toward a participative system of treatment and a consultative or participative system of making management decisions, while reserving important policy decisions for the superintendent. An important step was to communicate to lower level personnel the differences between making decisions and providing input for decisions. The strategy involved using a management team to make management decisions and treatment teams to make treatment decisions, with a linking pin (members of management) being part of both teams. We felt that as a participative Management by Objectives (MBO) program would be consistent with the overall consultative/participative system it could strengthen and support the institution.

The plan became more precise when a distinction between management decisions and treatment decisions was made. The treatment teams were given the authority to prescribe for and supervise the treatment team of the juveniles and thus felt responsible for their treatment. Overall policy decisions were made by the management team (composed of the superintendent, assistant superintendent, and department heads), within the limits of the framework dictated from above (the agency's goals, policies, and standards). The "ideal" management system was participative in regard to overall policy guidelines, management decisions, and treatment decisions.

The idea of linkage between the management team and treatment teams is shown in Figure 2. The role of the linking pin would be to clarify policy and approve decisions. The treatment team would have formal authority to make treatment decisions (not merely recommendations) for individual juveniles and, through the linking pin, would provide input to the management team on a continuing basis.

While the agency personnel desired a relatively equal distribution of influence, we felt that, because of the nature and recruitment of personnel and the orientation of the lower level personnel toward accepting responsibility, it would not be possible to develop a fully participative system (System 4). A consultative system (or high System 3) seemed to be a more appropriate and realistic objective.[1]

Site B

The prescription for Site B was to utilize a straight-line centralized system for both treatment and management. There were two centralized

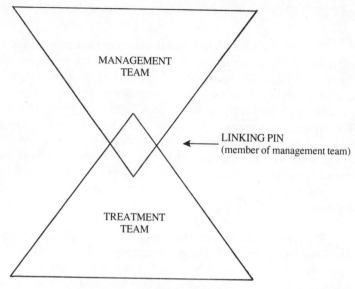

FIGURE 2
Recommended Ideal Linkage Between
Management and Treatment Teams

committees composed of upper level managers, which made treatment decisions, subject to the approval of the superintendent and the assistant superintendent. Upward communication was structured and formalized through written reports, which provided the basis for treatment decisions made at the top level. Since participation and decentralization did not fit this diagnosis, we moved to de-emphasize these concepts. We did not recommend MBO.

At Site B the modified behavior modification treatment system dictated consistency in treatment of the delinquent youth. The most appropriate management system was one which helped produce the consistency of a centralized, structured, and formalized system with standardized policies and rules guiding the rehabilitation of the delinquents. Again we were matching the requirements of the treatment system (technology) and the management system.

Developing our theory required a combination of institution and logical analysis. The goal was to match and develop consistency in the subsystems, choosing participation or nonparticipation as appropriate. Although our personal bias was for participation, theory rather than personal bias must guide management practice.

APPLICATION OF THE THEORETICAL MODEL TO GUIDE THE ORGANIZATION DEVELOPMENT EFFORTS IN THE INSTITUTIONS

Site A

Although in initial discussions top level management expressed a strong belief in participation, a survey of the managerial and professional staff showed this stated belief was not put into practice. The lower level professionals did not feel adequately involved in the decision-making process. Our major objective was to develop consistency between the expressed participative philosophy of the top administrators and the day-to-day practice of this philosophy. The principal strategy for meeting this objective was a regularly scheduled seminar conducted over a six-month period attended on a voluntary basis by top level management and professional staff. The seminar was supplemented by informal conferences and telephone calls.

The survey results (supplemented by small brain-storming groups) showed that the major problem centered on decision making and the role of the treatment teams in decision making. The treatment teams had been making decisions and formalizing rehabilitation programs for the delinquent youth but their decisions had sometimes been overruled by the superintendent. The result was that treatment teams began to simply "go through the motions" and the overruling of their decisions became more and more frequent. The solution to this problem was the development and systematic use of a procedure for downward communication and feedback, through which the groups received explanations of the rationale for the overruling of decisions.

We found that values had to be introduced sequentially and timed in implementation in order to develop consistency of philosophy, skills, and practice. We now feel that because lower level personnel are not willing to take full responsibility for their participation, a consultative (System 3) rather than a fully participative (System 4) system is appropriate. As top management cannot delegate responsibility, we feel a consultative system is also more appropriate for their needs, since in extreme cases treatment decisions must be overruled.

Site B

The diagnosis and change strategies at Site B differed from those at Site A, although the institutions were of comparable size and in the same state system. Our theory was that a centralized management system was appropriate at Site B and the management at that institution was already systematically moving in that direction. The recommendation for Site B was to refine and strengthen the evolving system. Fairness toward the delinquents in enforcement of rules, together with the modified behavior modification program, dictated the need for consistency rather than the individualized treatment required by the positive peer culture at Site A. Having a different theory led us to different recommendations and to a lower level of consultant involvement, especially in terms of our time. Our involvement at Site B consisted of initial orientation, survey administration, and feedback of results, with specific action planning to solve identified problems and make refinements. The change strategy included: (1) formalizing in writing the ways to treat and act toward the juveniles; (2) enforcing these rules and regulations consistently and fairly; (3) teaching the logic and methods of carrying out the treatment philosophy (through formal classes and informally); and (4) listening and giving positive encouragement to staff at all levels.

Since MBO implies decentralization and individual goals, it was inconsistent with the treatment system at Site B. We therefore advised management that participative MBO was not worth the cost and time for implementation and administration. We recommended that in this institution MBO be defined as refining and better stating the institution's objectives.

SUMMARY

The thesis of this paper is that neither participative/decentralized nor nonparticipative/centralized strategies are applicable in all rehabilitation agencies. We found that the treatment methodology is a moderating variable in correctional institutions. In these institutions treatment systems should be matched with management systems to develop consistency. In this way efficiency and effectiveness can be improved, whether the systems be participative or nonparticipative.

Since our paper is based on experience in only two institutions, some caution must be used in generalizing our results. However, we urge the development and use in all situations of managerial practice based on theory.

FOOTNOTES

1. Rensis Likert, *The Human Organization* (New York: McGraw-Hill, 1967).

INFORMATION SYSTEMS
IN HUMAN SERVICE ORGANIZATIONS

Thomas P. Holland

Human service organizations face increasing demands from consumer groups and funding sources for greater accountability. In both public and private agencies, the acceptance of traditional operating procedures is declining and organizations are required to evaluate their programs against explicit performance criteria. Often there are differences of opinion on the results a program is intended to produce as well as on the choice of relevant outcome indicators. At the same time, there is a belief that modification of existing procedures and implementation of new ones will bring an organization closer to the achievement of its goals.

In order to improve health, educational, and welfare services, planners are developing extensive procedures for obtaining and utilizing information about targeted human needs and preferences. They are also monitoring and assessing the impacts of alternative approaches. Findings must then be transmitted to managers for use in modifying and reshaping programs. The processes of collecting, processing, and utilizing such information are crucial to the design and management of more effective services.

In practice, however, managers' decisions seem often to be made on the basis of quite limited information. New information and knowledge often go unrecognized and technically magnificent systems for information retrieval go unused. The field of information systems has extensively addressed the issues of data collection, processing, and presentation. Actual utilization, however, has not been so successfully demonstrated.

Originally developed to perform repetitive tasks on large batches of simple figures, data processing systems have been greatly expanded to deal with much more complex types of information. Their potential for contributing to macro-level planning and management decisions was soon recognized. An elaborate processing technology developed, with the capacity for measuring, storing, and printing out data on a vast range of variables. Unfortunately, the technology seems to have advanced far more rapidly than the ability to use it effectively. It is no secret that widespread disillusionment with the use of automated data systems has caused them to be critically viewed. Hopefully, such experiences will lead to more realistic expectations of what these systems can be expected to contribute to the planning, management, and evaluation of human service programs.

The author's experiences in developing and trying to sustain computer-based information systems led to an interest in the all too frequent problem of breakdown after a system has been carefully designed and installed. Reams of print-out fill the shelves but have little impact on staff, except perhaps to aggravate their burdens of collecting and processing the data. What can be done to make the technology more useful?

The literature on the use of information systems in management describes numerous rational and normative models. Many of these rest upon the questionable assumptions that: (1) an organization has a single objective toward which all activities are oriented; and (2) decisions are made with perfect or near perfect knowledge of options and consequences.[1] Neither assumption accurately describes the functioning of most human service organizations. Other models approach this area at a less abstract level by first assuming the limitations of automated data processing systems and then considering how managers should adapt themselves to use the technology efficiently.[2]

The influences and constraints upon managers seem to be far more complex than is generally recognized in such literature. Improving capabilities for processing and utilizing information in a human service organization requires much more than the simple importation of a pre-packaged M.I.S. Such systems appear to have been oversold to harried managers eager to bring order to their jobs. It is now time to re-examine our use of information systems in the light of the realities of the organizational context in which decisions are made and implemented.

SOME LESSONS FROM INDUSTRY

Although it has seldom been noted, many efforts to develop and implement information systems in industry have failed. Many corporations have given up after a number of attempts to set such systems up and their experiences can be instructive. Krauss[3] reviewed a number of studies and described some reasons for the failures:

1. orienting the system to the computer rather than to the users
2. underestimating the complexity of the management situation or of the development of the system
3. lack of enthusiastic support and participation by top management

4. lack of dependable or reliable data sources

5. relying on outside consultants having little stake in the results of the system

6. lack of standard definitions of terms used in identifying data

7. requiring extensive use of codes by staff rather than by the data processing center

8. using codes rather than English titles in the output reports

9. lack of adequate communication and understanding of the nature and purpose of the system.

This list could go on and the industrial situations in which these problems have been successfully resolved are discouragingly few. In cases where information systems were successful, Krauss maintains that all of the following conditions were met:

1. The process began with management and staff recognizing that an information problem existed and that they wanted to do something about it.

2. Line management, not lateral staff, were given responsibility for the analysis of the problem and for the specification of the criteria for solving it.

3. The initial focus of application was in a critical action-oriented area of the business, such as product or service delivery, not in budgeting or accounting.

4. The information problem was approached first by defining the content, format, and timing of the end-need rather than by nonselectively attacking the mass of available data. Each need was given a relative priority to prevent the technicians from getting bogged down in minutiae.

5. Once the end-need was defined and a priority given, the place where the required information was first available was identified and a method of capturing the information at that point was established.

6. Once information was entered into the system, all needs for it across the organization were serviced from one record. Other reports were eliminated unless they served a function which could be served in no other way.

7. All input and output were recorded in a form and language easily understood by everyone.

8. The users of the system had a clear understanding of the nature and purpose of the system and its benefits to them.

The advocates of transferring information systems into the human services often gloss over the numerous problems of implementation. They make assumptions about the nature of management and the use of information which are no more true in industry than they are in human service agencies. Some of the common assumptions are described by Krauss:[4]

1. Decision makers can readily state what information they need in order to be more effective. This is a very difficult problem. Even if a manager can specify his problem areas, it does not follow that he knows what information should be brought to bear on them. Systems developers who have expected executives in any sort of organization to set forth their requirements in clear terms have almost always been disappointed.

2. Decisions will improve as more information is made available. Several faults can be seen in this assumption. Obviously, more information of the wrong kind will help no one. Also, the mere presence of an abundance of information will not help without some method of selecting what is relevant to the problem at hand. The sheer bulk of information only makes it harder to differentiate the relevant from the irrelevant.

3. Managers are starving for information. This is one of the most obviously invalid assumptions. If anything, managers suffer from an overload of information. What is needed is simplification: a method of delivering the appropriate information in the form and at the time it is needed.

4. Managers need information faster. This assumption appears to be valid, but its validity depends on the kind of decision to be made and the kind of information needed to make it. Long-range planning decisions do not require the same quick timing as, for example, the assignment of new tasks to workers.

From experience in industry, it is clear that the basic issue in the development of a useful information system is not the technology but the accurate analysis of managers' information needs. An information system is not being implanted in a void. Every manager has methods, however simple or complex, for getting and using the information he needs. Unfortunately, instead of attempting to improve these methods, many corporations have imported whole new systems bearing little relation to existing procedures. The technically controlled approach too often looks at what *should* be happening rather than at feasible ways of improving what *is* happening. Technically elegant systems are often totally impractical and are therefore seldom used. The disillusionment that follows their failure often leads to cynicism about any information system.

We now turn our attention to the complex issues of adapting information systems to the distinctive needs of human service organizations.

ADAPTING INFORMATION SYSTEMS FOR
HUMAN SERVICE PROGRAMS

Recent efforts in adapting information systems technology have focused on the development of methods for providing managers with information which is relevant to the issues they confront. This requirement has meant that information systems for human service programs must differ in several basic ways from traditional systems. They must be based on the needs and processes of management in human service agencies. They must collect, process, and present information in forms useful to various levels of administration. They must document the achievements or results of services as well as the procedures of service delivery.

Interest in such systems has drawn from two areas of research and experience in human service programs. One area is that of social planning and organizational administration. The other is the increasingly important one of the application of quantitative reporting and evaluation procedures to human service programs. The convergence of these two streams has focused attention on the need for information systems which are responsive to the processes of decision making and supportive of the effective management of large-scale service systems at local and regional levels.[5]

Information Needs of Human Service Managers

The thrust toward decentralization of allocation and planning functions for human services has placed increased responsibility and demands for accountability upon local and regional planning bodies as well as upon direct service agencies. Howland,[6] in his attempt to conceptualize a community health system, emphasized three different levels of decision making which must be considered. The *strategic* level is concerned with policy formation, goal setting, and resource allocation. The *operational* level is concerned with implementation of policy through long- and short-range program planning and monitoring. The *tactical* level is concerned with the implementation of the programmatic components which have been developed to operationalize strategic level policy. The constant monitoring of service delivery activities, as well as the maintenance of an organization and of a staff who are "on the firing line" to deliver services, are the principal functions of the tactical level.

Within this basic decision structure of human service systems, various patterns have emerged, both in the development of local service delivery systems and in the development of the decision-making and planning bodies responsible for those systems. The establishment of these patterns has been influenced by such variable factors as the extent of available services, community support for them, and legal and fiscal requirements. The multi-agency council and the regional, county, or metropolitan planning approach represent some of the ways undertaken to develop comprehensive service systems.

There are many issues that shape what managers at strategic, operational, and tactical levels must consider in their respective roles. Programmatic information may include such areas as the following:

1. objectives (in terms of client or population achievement) which are being pursued by the system
2. service delivery patterns which are being implemented to achieve these objectives
3. priorities of various community constituents concerning the need for pursuing these versus other objectives
4. professional and lay orientations toward human services of different types
5. managerial and organizational factors which affect the delivery of these services on a community-wide basis.

Each kind of information represents an area of which a decision maker must be aware. Information systems for the human services have concentrated on reporting of voluminous data on program processes (service delivery statistics), while at times neglecting information on the achievement of program objectives. A method is needed of providing decision makers with a more complete range of information displayed in useable form and with assistance in utilizing it systematically.

When the utilization and potential of information systems technology in the human services are assessed, some disconcerting trends are evident. For one thing, these managers have unsatisfied needs for a wide variety of decision-related information. The National Academy of Public Administration's study[7] on multi-agency mental health programs noted, for example, that: "Systematic analysis of catchment area needs was not being carried out in any of the nine centers visited." This study recommended that the National Institute of Mental Health should require and support the development of center staff capability to conduct epidemiological surveys and analyses and to perform program analyses necessary to provide feedback on the effectiveness of center programs. Furthermore, this same study emphasized that:

If a community mental health center is to exercise rational choice in developing a balanced program of services directed to the most acute needs of its catchment area, then the center must start with a reporting system which provides accurate timely data on needs and services provided by categories. If NIMH is to act intelligently in developing national policies on mental health and administering grant-in-aid programs to implement these policies, then it must have access to comparable program data on all community health centers in operation.

Unfortunately, although managers in human service programs require a variety of information, not all the information they receive will be decision-relevant. On the contrary, they run a serious risk of being inundated by the information produced by various systems. It has been known for some time that it is easy to subject an individual decision maker to "information overload."[8] It is no more true in the human services than in industry that the more information collected and disseminated, the better the resulting decisions. If the human services decision maker receives too much information he may make poorer decisions than he would have made with little information at all.

We are repeating in the human services the cycle of developmental problems that industry has already faced. The root of this difficulty seems to be the absence of early and ongoing contact between decision makers and information producers. If information is defined and collected without adequate involvement of its potential users, it will have little impact on decisions. Speaking about one information model, Schulberg and Baker[9] have commented that "never having meant to attain the goal studied by the researcher, the administrator sees no need to alter his program to accommodate the researcher." Walker[10] has noted that an information system will have no impact on the organization if it does not provide for consequences which will result in the development and maintenance of desirable staff behaviors. In a slightly different vein, Rivlin[11] has pointed out that limiting to a single valued measure of performance the amount of information upon which decisions are to be made involves dangers, too, most notably those of constricting decision makers and removing incentives.

Another fact that cannot be ignored in assessing the utilization of information systems in multi-level decision making in the human services is the threat they present to decision makers at the level of service delivery operations. If all levels do not participate in the design of the system and come to an agreement on its purposes and content, utilization is unlikely.

The research team involved in the design and implementation of an evaluation and information system at the Jewish Community Federation of Cleveland described this resistance in terms of:

> . . . *the agencies' real and rational fear of being measured. In a semi-autonomous system of agencies such as the JCF, each agency looks at the model from its own unique viewpoint and assesses the model's cost and utility* to the agency. [12]

Since service delivery personnel will ultimately be responsible for producing much of the information system's input, it is not surprising that failure to deal with resistance at this level has led to the untimely demise of many information systems. Involvement of appropriate individuals, rather than technical feasibility, is thus the key issue in the human services just as in industry. The newer approaches emphasize such involvement. Educational and technical assistance and other supportive devices must be aimed at ensuring that past inadequacies of information systems are not perpetuated. When this emphasis is coupled with an explicit attempt to recognize *all levels* of decision making and their unique characteristics, the resulting product should be much sounder and more useful to decision makers in any human service organization.

Some Conditions for Success

Comparisons of successful and unsuccessful information systems in human service programs indicate a number of conditions necessary for a system's survival. As described by O'Brien and Service, [13] these conditions parallel many of the concerns expressed in the literature about management problems in human service programs and the past ineffectiveness of information systems in resolving these problems:

1. *The information must be really used, not just collected and forgotten.* A system which will gather information for decision making and planning will get the support of agencies. If such a system also reduces the total amount of time spent on data gathering and reporting it should be received even more favorably by agencies.

2. *Evaluation of programs must focus both on outcome of service and on processes of service delivery.* An evaluation system which examines only the accomplishments of a service program would be inadequate as a tool for operational-level consultation with agencies on how to increase effectiveness. It would also be too sudden a change of perspective for most agencies.

3. *One must set realistic outcome expectations for short-range objectives*. The system cannot reward the setting of unrealistically high outcome objectives and the delivery of relatively low performance on those objectives. The importance or priority of accomplishing a particular outcome objective must be weighed against the likelihood that the agency will achieve it.

4. *The system should help to clarify (for operational and strategic as well as tactical levels) the social value, personnel, ideological, and fiscal constraints under which programs must be operated*. To be useful an information system must be able to provide explicit information about factors which foster or hinder the achievement of program outcome objectives.

5. *In high priority areas, the system should allow for the modification of outcome objectives for demonstration or experimental programs*. A system of decision-relevant information must be able to consider the experimental nature of new program efforts.

6. *The system must provide information relevant to individual programs but in a form comparable across different types of programs and agencies*. Use of information for planning, consultation, and allocation purposes requires varied forms of presentation. The system must be able to produce a variety of output matched to the needs of the individual users.

7. *The system must provide data for planning purposes*. A realistic information system must permit a focus on the planning of a total pattern of human services for the area and must also provide data for external reporting regarding the pattern of services.

8. *The system cannot make decisions but must support decision making by those who are responsible for it*. The information system should rely upon multiple indicators which not only allow responsible decision makers the latitude they need to consider various constraints, but also permit the information to be used for more than one purpose.

9. *The system must provide information for documenting service needs and setting priorities*. To facilitate the determination of priorities the information system should provide the means for systematic collection and display of data on service needs, both for internal use and for presentation to outside groups.

With these conditions for acceptance and utilization met, it is possible to develop systems for information reporting which can be truly helpful for planning and management at all levels. Let us turn now to an examination of the development and implementation of such systems.

APPROACHES TO SYSTEM DESIGN

The development of a useful management information system begins with a detailed analysis of decisions managers make and the information they presently use and need in order to make them. As Krauss[14] points out, there are two basic ways to conduct this analysis and to begin the development of a system: a data-based approach and a decision-based approach. Each approach has its contribution, and in fact any system is a mixture of both approaches. However, we shall attempt to build the case for a primary emphasis on the decision-based perspective.

The Data-Based Approach

Proponents of this approach are numerous and usually are technically oriented. The methodology consists of gathering whatever data may exist in the organization and storing them in a computer. The forms and records which are being used are routed through the information center and the data entered into the computer's memory bank. Thus, at least in theory, management has on hand whatever data it has already decided it needs for running the organization. Technicians organize the data so that they can be recalled in numerous forms and put to almost any conceivable use. Extremely flexible output is then promised to anyone who wants it. This approach is justified on the grounds that being prepared for nearly any situation, even an unknown one, has benefits which exceed the costs of storing an excessive volume of data which may never be used.[15]

As should be apparent, this approach bypasses the whole issue of the *use* of the system. It is like building a vast library of everything in print and announcing that the answers to your questions are here if you want to come and look. Too often it seems that the answer you need is not in the library, which is also terrifically expensive to maintain. If any system is to be applicable to the organization's priorities and values, management must be very specific initially about the kinds of data it wants. As one information systems developer[16] observed:

> *The desire for information is essentially unlimited, but the necessity for paying cold cash for it will force a scale of relative values to*

be established. Since the costs of using the system must be com-
pared to the values the user receives, this comparison will be a vital
part of the user's thinking during the systems development process,
as he attempts to distinguish his wants from his real needs.

The Decision-Based Approach

This approach focuses on the decisions being made by managers, identifying the information they use and need to use to make those decisions. It then seeks the most efficient and least disruptive method of getting that information to those people in the form they need and when they need it.

The most difficult and complex part of this approach is the analysis of the decisions and the requirements, constraints, and needs surrounding them. The process begins with getting a thorough understanding of the participants' objectives, underlying values, policies and directives, plans for the future, and daily operating procedures. It includes careful attention to the specific work performed, the categories of that work, the kinds of demands on each manager, the volume of work, sequences, timing, and trends of change in the managers' jobs. It also must carefully consider the rules governing operations. These usually can be expressed in "if . . . then" statements: if the applications for a given type of service exceed some amount per month or quarter, then some decision about staff allocation is to be made by the program manager. Or: if expenditures in a certain category exceed some amount, then a decision has to be made about future limits.

Information Needs Analysis

The analysis of information needed to make decisions can begin at various points in the organization. The flow of information and communication through an organization is a complex process and rests largely on informal networks of relationships. These relationships must be taken into consideration in understanding the needs of and constraints on managers.

One effective way to obtain perspectives on information flow is what some people have called the "top-down" approach.[17] Starting with the board or policy-making group, moving to the executive, on to middle management, and then to the front-line staff, one sees how overall policies are sequentially translated into more and more specific activities. At each step along the way, the information needs are identified and the source of information noted. Particular attention is given to an activity at any level which does not clearly feed into an expectation at the level above.

The alternate approach is to begin at the "bottom" and work up. One of the strongest arguments for this is that a great deal of knowledge can be gained about how the organization really operates before talking with managers about how it *should* operate. A thorough knowledge of present conditions and where breakdowns occur can be extremely useful in discussions with top management on the organization's needs. On the other hand, it may be that management is aware of certain problems and has elected to focus on other priorities. It may also be that collecting fragments of information without any prior framework might produce a misunderstanding about the organization and negative reactions from top managers when the situation is finally discussed with them.

Some combination of these approaches seems important, allowing an understanding of the priorities at the top, the daily needs on the front line, and the flow of information between them. A map of the flow of information can be a useful device in the information needs analysis.

Another aspect of this analysis is that of the cost and effectiveness of present methods of obtaining and communicating information in the organization. It may be that the present way of coping with a given area is quite satisfactory and should be left alone, or it may be that the present way is the best *feasible* way, since any improvement would cost more than it could be worth. The focus then shifts to what unfulfilled or partially fulfilled information needs can be resolved with the resources available.

Another somewhat more technical issue that managers must face is that of how the raw data will be put in a form suitable for use in making decisions. The computer can do all kinds of manipulations, but the rules must be established by its users. These rules include how the data will be ordered or organized (by worker, by client, by service category, by geographic area); how data will be summarized (by average dollar costs for types of services, by volume of services in each category, etc.); how they will be analyzed and compared (for example, what can legitimately be included when calculating the costs for a unit of service or when comparing the productivity of two offices?). Finally, decisions must be made on the use of and rules for evaluation: what are the criteria against which costs and productivity data will be compared? does management wish to receive a report when any one of these indicators goes below or above a set range of expectations? which services' data can legitimately be compared and over what time and with what consequences?

These complex questions must be confronted before the information system can be designed. Development can begin only when clear agreement is reached on:

1. what specific information is to be produced
2. how and when and to whom and in what forms it is to be delivered
3. how and when and by whom and in what forms it is to be collected
4. what the rules are which will govern the processing and converting of the data into forms directly useful for making decisions.

STEPS IN THE DEVELOPMENT PROCESS

Recognition of the Problem

There are a number of ways that organizations can strengthen their capacities to obtain, assess, and utilize information for decision making. Recognition by the organization's participants, particularly top administration, of the crucial influence of information on decisions and on the achievement of goals is an essential component of organizational development in this area. Without top-level support, efforts to improve the organization's information system are doomed.

Building Upon Existing Systems

The first priority should not be to develop a totally new information system but to improve the existing informal information handling procedures and strengthen the organization's decision-making processes. The initial focus should be on identifying the problems which make the existing system unsatisfactory.

While the designer may have plans for an elaborate system, few organizations can sustain the costs of its operation. The designer must therefore move at the organization's pace and develop incremental adjustments in the existing system. While the "grand design" may provide a general framework for his operations, the needs of others in the organization will constrain his contribution to a level they feel is acceptable and feasible.

Since an incremental approach reduces the needs for organizational change, it can also help reduce resistance to change. The frequency with which elaborate automated systems fall into disuse underscores the necessity for caution and for careful thought to the actual needs of the users. Despite their technical inelegance, incremental extensions of existing information handling procedures appear much more likely to survive and to be used. [18]

151

The frustration of the information system designer with this incompatibility between the "real" and the "ideal" must be acknowledged. For example, although the exchange of data and comparison of variables across organizations are important to the system designer and perhaps also to some state and federal planners, information for other purposes may have a higher priority for the administrator of a particular organization. Obviously, the resources necessary to implement the designer's objectives will be available only if more immediate organizational priorities are satisfied. Probably the best result to be hoped for is the slow improvement of decisions through the gradual application of systematic information to the issues at hand.

Another source of disillusionment with some formal information systems is their tendency to provide managers with large volumes of data on everything quantifiable while omitting qualitative information that may be highly relevant to decision making. This category includes such critical information as priorities and values in the external environment, internal capacity and performance indicators, and the more familiar service inputs and process factors,[19] factors which may be only partially quantifiable. Most administrators distrust information that purports to reduce decisions to single indicators. They protest that their situation is unique. It may be desirable to acknowledge frankly that there are some things a formal information system cannot do which will continue to depend on the administrator's judgment. Although a system can provide information on some factors routinely and on others on demand, when and how attention will be paid to such information will probably always be an administrative decision. A good system will provide what is needed when it is needed, with the recognition that its users will filter the output through numerous subjective screens.

Specifying Information Needs

The information development process should begin in a particular problem area of the organization. It should involve front-line staff in the detailed examination and analysis of decisions being made as well as of the nature, types, and sources of information currently utilized in handling the problem. The staff would then specify the information needed to facilitate a more satisfactory solution.

The analysis would locate potential sources of such needed information, and specify how, in what form, and to whom such information would be maximally useful. This process would include the internal monitoring of current operations and the collection of new information for extending the range of alternative responses available.[20] The resulting system might include only limited use of automated processes in combination with manual and individualized procedures.

Developing Collection and Processing Capacities

Having determined the nature and sources of needed and useful information, the developmental process would examine the organization's procedures for scanning, collecting, filtering, and routing information. Such analysis would locate the most appropriate points at which information might be gathered and determine the most efficient and effective methods for condensing and distributing it.[21] Wherever possible, such procedures should attempt to build up existing methods of handling information before making new demands upon personnel.

Information would be summarized and presented to users in forms that are readily understandable, relevant to their needs, and available on time to answer their questions.[22] Large amounts of quantifiable data may be handled by computerization but qualitative information is less amenable to automation and requires a more imaginative and individualized approach.

Following the design and initial implementation of new or revised information handling procedures, the development task is not complete without extensive testing and close monitoring. Breakdowns will occur in the early stages, particularly when the revised procedures involve extensive departures from prior practice. If the system is working well, its users should be strongly motivated to support it.[23]

Supporting Innovation

The programs of a human service organization should be responsive to changes in its environment and resulting changes in its goals. Specific resources should be allocated for continuous scanning of the environment to draw new knowledge and ideas into the organization. Informal reliance upon staff initiative or the organization's research department is not sufficient for bringing new information into most organizations.[24]

As Larsen and Nichols[25] report, the utilization of new information in human service organizations is strongly related to specific administrative policies that encourage and support innovation. Their studies indicate that a major source of innovative ideas is exposure to new information through such methods as attending conferences and workshops. New concepts lead to further interest in and attention to new information. The purposeful collection and communication of new information throughout an organization can bring about change by suggesting solutions to immediate problems and by raising the aspiration level of participants. This process can lead to the consideration of more effective and efficient methods for attaining the organization's goals.

SOME CONCLUDING THOUGHTS

The development of more effective human services requires close attention to information gathering, processing, and utilization. These are shaped by the goals and values of the participants in the organization as well as by the problems and uncertainties inherent in providing services. When problems are encountered, a review of information and a search for new solutions are begun. Available alternatives are considered sequentially and filtered through the communications network of the organization and through the values of the participants.

In most organizations, the collection and use of information is an informal process and decision making is far from routine or even rational (in the usual sense of that term). The kinds of information most often used in planning and management decisions are usually not collected in any systematic manner and are only partially quantifiable. Examples of such information include individual values, benefits, priorities, previous experience with an activity, perceived capacity and readiness of staff to move, and consumer preferences. Most decision making is heavily influenced, if not determined, by political and value factors. They are oriented toward several objectives simultaneously, only some of which are overt, explicit, and consistent with other organizational goals.

Automated information systems usually involve the superimposition of a rational process on these quasi-rational procedures. Breakdowns occur where the quantitative and routinized aspects of the technical system do not meet the qualitative needs of decision makers. In order to be more effective, systems designers must have a more holistic view of organizational functioning and a more realistic expectation of where and to what extent decision making can be enhanced by automated data systems. They must be sensitive in analyzing the information needs of organizational users prior to designing and introducing new procedures.

Strengthening and extending systems require a detailed examination of decision-making points in the organization and a specification of the nature and types of information needed at each point. Such systems will include a range of information — objective and subjective, quantitative and qualitative. The procedures for collecting and processing information will include both formal, routinized and informal, individualized components. This approach to the development of information systems requires a wide range of technical, administrative, and social science skills. Both the administrator and the technical expert have valuable contributions to make.

The development of multi-faceted systems for scanning, collecting, transmitting, and using a variety of information will produce a more extensive range of alternatives for decision making. Management effectiveness can be strengthened through the availability of new options for choice. The systematic utilization of this new knowledge can serve to enhance and guide operational change.

FOOTNOTES

1. W. Edwards and A. Tversky, eds., *Decision Making* (Baltimore: Penguin Books, 1967); A.G. Papandreou, "Some Basic Problems in the Theory of the Firm," in *A Survey of Contemporary Economics,* ed. B.F. Haley (Homewood, Ill.: Richard D. Irwin, 1952).

2. R.W. Brady *et al., Administrative Data Processing: The Case for Executive Management Involvement* (Boulder, Co.: National Center for Higher Education Management Systems, 1975).

3. L.I. Krauss, *Computer-Based Management Information Systems* (New York: American Management Association, 1970), pp. 24-27.

4. Ibid.; pp. 41-45.

5. G.M. O'Brien and A.L. Service, "A Decision Support System for Community Mental Health," Unpublished Manuscript, Human Services Design Laboratory, School of Applied Social Sciences, Case Western Reserve University, 1973.

6. D. Howland, "Toward a Community Health System Model," in *Systems and Medical Care,* eds., A. Sheldon, F. Baker, and C. McLaughlin (Cambridge, Mass.: M.I.T. Press, 1970).

7. National Academy of Public Administration, *The Multi-Agency Community Mental Health Center: Administrative and Organizational Relationships* (Washington, D.C.: NAPA, 1971).

8. G.A. Miller, "The Magical Number Seven, Plus or Minus Two: Some Limits on our Capacity for Processing Information," *Psychological Review* (1956): 81-97.

9. H. Schulberg and F. Baker, "Program Evaluation Models and the Implementation of Research Findings," *American Journal of Public Health* 58 (1968): 1248-55.

10. R.A. Walker, "The Ninth Panacea: Program Evaluation," *Evaluation* 1 (Fall 1972): 45-53.

11. A.M. Rivlin, *Systematic Thinking for Social Action* (Washington, D.C.: The Brookings Institution, 1971).

12. S.J. Mantel, Jr. *et al.,* "A Social Service Measurement Model," Technical Memorandum, Department of Operations Research, Case Western Reserve University, Cleveland, Ohio, January 1973.

13. O'Brien and Service, 1973.

14. Krauss, 1970.

15. Ibid., pp. 73-75.

16. S.C. Blumenthal, *Management Information Systems: A Framework for Planning and Development* (Englewood Cliffs, N.J.: Prentice-Hall, 1969).

17. Krauss, 1970, pp. 77-78.

18. J. Dearden, "How to Organize Information Systems," *Harvard Business Review* 43 (1965): 65-73.

19. O'Brien and Service, 1973; S.A. Spencer, "The Dark at the Top of the Stairs," *Management Review* 51 (1962): 4-12.

20. D.R. Daniel, "Management Information Crisis," *Harvard Business Review* 39 (1961): 111-121.

21. Dearden, 1965.

22. O'Brien and Service, 1973.

23. Spencer, 1962.

24. E.M. Glaser, "Knowledge Transfer and Institutional Change," Unpublished Manuscript, Human Interaction Research Institute, Los Angeles, Ca.

25. J.K. Larsen and D.G. Nichols, "If Nobody Knows You've Done It, Have You?" *Evaluation* 1 (1972): 39-44.

REFERENCES

Berger, P.L., and Luckmann, T. *The Social Construction of Reality*. New York: Anchor, 1967.

Blumenthal, S.C. *Management Information Systems: A Framework for Planning and Development*. Englewood Cliffs, N.J.: Prentice-Hall, 1969.

Boulding, K., ed. *Conflict Management in Organizations*. Ann Arbor: Foundation for Research on Human Behavior, 1961.

Brady, R.W. *et al*. *Administrative Data Processing: The Case For Executive Management Involvement*. Boulder, Co.: National Center for Higher Education Management Systems, 1975.

Charnes, A., and Cooper, W.W. "The Theory of Search: Optimum Distribution of Search Effort." *Management Science* 5 (1959): 44-50.

Coser, R.L. "Authority and Decision Making in a Hospital." *American Sociological Review* 23(1) (1958): 56-63.

Cyert, R.M., and March, J.G. *A Behavioral Theory of the Firm*. Englewood Cliffs, N.J.: Prentice-Hall, 1964.

Daniel, D.R. "Management Information Crisis." *Harvard Business Review* 39 (1961): 111-21.

Dearden, J. "How to Organize Information Systems." *Harvard Business Review* 43 (1965): 65-73.

Edwards, W., and Tversky, A., eds. *Decision Making*. Baltimore: Penguin Books, 1967.

Etzioni, A. *Modern Organizations*. Englewood Cliffs, N.J.: Prentice-Hall, 1964.

Glaser, E.M. "Knowledge Transfer and Institutional Change." Unpublished Manuscript. Human Interaction Research Institute, Los Angeles, California.

Guetzkow, H. "Conversion Barriers in Using the Social Sciences." *Administrative Science Quarterly* 4(1) (1959): 68-81.

Havelock, R.G. *Planning for Innovation Through Dissemination and Utilization of Knowledge*. Ann Arbor: University of Michigan, 1970.

Havelock, R.G. "Research Utilization in Four Federal Agencies." Paper presented at the Annual Meeting, American Psychological Association, Honolulu, Hawaii, 1971.

Howland, D. "Toward a Community Health System Model." In *Systems and Medical Care*. Edited by A. Sheldon, F. Baker, and C. McLaughlin. Cambridge, Mass.: M.I.T. Press, 1970.

Katz, D., and Kahn, R.L. *The Social Psychology of Organizations*. New York: Wiley, 1966.

Kiresuk, T.J., and Sherman, R.E. "Goal Attainment Scaline: A General Method for Evaluating Comprehensive Community Mental Health Programs." *Community Mental Health Journal* 4 (1968): 443-53.

Kitchel, J.M., ed. *Knowledge Production and Utilization in Educational Administration*. Eugene, Oregon: Center for the Advanced Study of Educational Administration, 1968.

Krauss, L.I. *Computer-Based Management Information Systems*. New York: American Management Association, 1970.

Larsen, J.K., and Nichols, D.G. "If Nobody Knows You've Done It, Have You?" *Evaluation* 1 (1972): 39-44.

Lindblom, C.E. *The Intelligence of Democracy: Decision Making Through Mutual Adjustment*. New York: Free Press, 1965.

Manneheim, K. *Ideology and Utopia*. New York: Harcourt, Brace, 1952.

Mantel, S.J., Jr. *et al.* "A Social Service Measurement Model." Technical Memorandum, Department of Operations Research, Case Western Reserve University, Cleveland, Ohio, January 1973.

March, J.G., and Simon, H. A. *Organizations*. New York: Wiley, 1967.

McDonough, A.M. *Information Economics and Management Science*. New York: McGraw-Hill, 1963.

McRae, T.W., ed. *Management Information Systems*. Baltimore, Penguin Books, 1971.

Miller, G.A. "The Magical Number Seven, Plus or Minus Two: Some Limits on our Capacity for Processing Information." *Psychological Review* (1956): 81-97.

Murdick, R.G., and Ross, J.E. *Information Systems for Modern Management*. Englewood Cliffs, N.J.: Prentice-Hall, 1971.

National Academy of Public Administration. *The Multi-Agency Community Mental Health Center: Administrative and Organizational Relationships*. Washington, D.C.: NAPA, 1971.

O'Brien, G.M. "Research Utilization in Program Design." *Welfare in Review* 10(2) (1972): 1-10.

O'Brien, G.M., and Service, A.L. "A Decision Support System for Community Mental Health." Unpublished Manuscript. Human Services Design Laboratory, School of Applied Social Sciences, Case Western Reserve University, 1973.

Papandreou, A.G. "Some Basic Problems in the Theory of the Firm." In *A Survey of Contemporary Economics*. Edited by B.F. Haley. Homewood, Ill.: Richard D. Irwin, 1952.

Perrow, C. *Organizational Analysis: A Sociological View*. Belmont, California: Wadsworth, 1970.

Rivlin, A.M. *Systematic Thinking For Social Action*. Washington, D.C.: The Brookings Institution, 1971.

Schulberg, H., and Baker, F. "Program Evaluation Models and the Implementation of Research Findings." *American Journal of Public Health* 58 (1968): 1248-55.

Shaw, M.E. "Some Effects of Unequal Distribution of Information Upon Group Performance in Various Communication Nets." *Journal of Social Psychology* 49 (1954): 547-53.

Simon, H.A. *Administrative Behavior*. New York: Macmillan, 1957.

Simon, H.A. "A Behavioral Model of Rational Choice." *Quarterly Journal of Economics* 69 (1955): 99-118.

Spencer, S.A. "The Dark at the Top of the Stairs." *Management Review* 51 (1962): 4-12.

Street, D.; Vinter, R.D.; and Perrow, C. *Organization of Treatment*. New York: Free Press, 1966.

Taylor, D.W. "Decision Making and Problem Solving." In *Handbook of Organizations*. Edited by J.G. March. Chicago: Rand-McNally, 1965.

Thomas, J.H., and Bennis, W.G., eds. *Management of Change and Conflict*. Baltimore: Penguin Books, 1972.

Walker, R.A. "The Ninth Panacea: Program Evaluation." *Evaluation* 1 (Fall 1972): 45-53.

Welsch, L.A., and Cyert, R.M., eds. *Management Decision Making*. Baltimore: Penguin Books, 1971.

REPRESENTING AN ORGANIZATION IN THE MANAGEMENT OF HUMAN SERVICES

Richard Ford

Man is a social animal with a propensity for organizing and managing his affairs. He does so in an increasingly complex and dynamic environment. Many disciplines are contributing to an eclectic body of knowledge — organization theory — which, coupled with experience, is the foundation for practice![1]

The tendency to organize, to join together to accomplish those goals and objectives which only coordination of human and material resources can achieve, is as old as the history of mankind. Man first organized and managed his affairs in family units, then in tribes and communities, and later in more complex social, economic, and political units.

Management thought, rooted in antiquity as it may be, has experienced most of its growth in the twentieth century. The introduction of science, the study of functions, the experimentation with human behavior, the recognition of the human factor, and the introduction of social systems concepts and contingency analysis are just over fifty years old.

While systems theory is not new, the systems analysis approach now in vogue emphasizes the direct study and analysis of management as an open system, a concept which is relatively new in the field of management studies. Simply stated, the systems approach postulates the interrelationship and interdependence of system elements, which in interaction form a unitary whole. In management analysis, systems are viewed as general or specialized and closed or open. A general system would include such elements as formal organization and philosophical concepts. A specialized system would include such areas as organization structure planning and information budgeting systems. A closed system has no external input and emphasizes internal relationships and consistency. An open system is an energetic input-output system which interacts with the environment. [2]

While open systems may differ in some characteristics, Katz and Kahn[3] have defined nine factors which seem to be common to all:

1. the *input of energy* from the external environment
2. the *through-put* process of transforming available energy into a product

3. the *out-put* of exporting a product into the environment

4. *re-cycles of events* furnish the sources of energy for the repetition of the cycle of activities

5. *negative entropy* moves to arrest the process of entropy, that universal law in which an organization moves toward disorganization or death

6. the *feedback* of information helps the system maintain a steady state

7. *dynamic homeostasis* counteracts entropy and moves toward growth and expansion

8. *differentiation* and *elaboration* are the tendencies for organizations to move toward elaboration roles with greater specialization of functions

9. *equifinality* is the characteristic by which a system can reach the same final state from differing initial conditions and by a variety of paths.

Some theorists have criticized the most current open systems approach because, while it emphasizes the input of the environment, it does not relate the environment functionally to management concepts. The contingency approach to management has attempted to continue from the point at which systems analysis stops.

The contingency approach emphasizes the relationship of function to the independent variable of environment. The basic theme is that there is no best way of designing jobs and/or organizations, managing people, and changing organizations. Hellriegel and Slocum[4] present four major parts of the overall conceptual framework for contingency management. They are:

1. environmental properties
2. individual properties
3. organizational properties
4. group properties

''The relationships between these major areas are much too dynamic to allow us to set forth 'laws' about their relationships.''[5] Different organizations, with different tasks and different competitive environments, require different sets of plans, all of which may change with changes in demands from any one of the areas.

In the opinion of the writer, the contingency approach holds the most promise for the future development and effective analysis of management practice. The most significant reason for this assumption is that the contingency framework can incorporate all other management approaches.

Representing the organization — advancing its interests through contacts with the task environment outside the organization — is a management function which lends itself to the application of contingency analysis. In his role as representative of the organization, the manager must have a working knowledge of the internal and external systems within which he functions.

Taking the classical approach to management functions, as identified by Foyal, Taylor, Gulich, and others,[6] and applying the currently popular systems and contingency analysis to these functions, it is possible to develop a comprehensive perspective of the role of management in representing.

All managers must take into account in varying degrees the elements and forces of their external environment. Kast and Rosenzweig[7] have identified two environmental areas that influence an organization:

    1. the societal (general) environment, which affects all organizations in a given society
    2. the specific (task) environment, which affects the individual organization more directly.

To give a detailed description of all the environmental variables that affect management in organizations would be an impossible task. Therefore, because of its relevance to specific organizations, greater attention will be given to the task environment. The distinction between the two environments is not always the same, since environment is a continuum on which what is relevant is a matter of degree. The environment is continually changing and the general areas move into the task areas of an organization.[8] Managers must, therefore, be responsive to their entire environment. They must identify, evaluate, and react to the forces external to the organization that may be relevant to its operation.

The forces in the general environment are difficult to identify and list; authors have classified a number of characteristics which may help in developing a framework for analysis of their influence on the organization. The following characteristics have been suggested:

    1. cultural — including ideologies, values, and norms
    2. technological — including scientific levels and technological advancement
    3. educational — including literacy and specialized training
    4. political — including concentration of power and party system
    5. legal — including laws and governmental units
    6. natural — including climatic and other conditions and resources
    7. demographic — including human resources, distribution by age, sex, etc.

8. sociological — including social roles and nature of organizational development
9. economic — including consumption characteristics and physical resources.[9]

Any one or a combination of the above factors may at any time move from the general to the task environment, becoming specifically relevant to the organization.

The task environment is different for each organization; however, there are some components which can be considered relevant to most human service organizations:

1. client-public component, including actual users and citizens generally
2. suppliers component, including labor and professional areas
3. competitor component, including inter-agency relationships and service demands
4. socio-political component, including government regulations and public attitudes
5. technological component, including new techniques and delivery systems.[10]

The study of an organization's task environment and its impact on the organization is relatively new. Thompson postulates that task environments also are characterized by two basic dimensions: homogeneous-heterogeneous and stable-dynamic. He shows how the boundary-spanning functions in an organization can be functionally differentiated to correspond to the organization's task environment. As an organization's environment becomes more heterogeneous, it brings greater constraints to the organization and demands a greater variety of functional skills and divisions in response. Also, as the environment becomes more dynamic, it forces more contingencies on the organization, leading to a higher degree of decentralization. With a heterogeneous and dynamic task environment, the boundary units would be expected to be functionally differentiated according to the relevant factors in the task environment, with each unit decentralized in order to monitor and respond to changes in its sector.[11]

Thus, the task environment concept identifies those factors in the environment which are relevant to the organization's goal setting and to the definition of its domain.

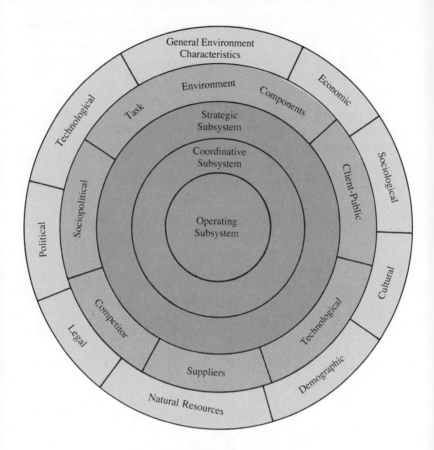

FIGURE 1
Relationship of General and Task Environments
to the Organizational System

Source: From *Organization and Management* by E.F. Kast and J.E. Rosen-zweig. Copyright 1970, McGraw-Hill. Used with permission of McGraw-Hill Book Company.

The general and task environments and their relationships to the organizational system are shown in Figure 1. These relationships suggest that most, if not all, of the environmental elements involve an accelerating rate of change. The figure shows also the strategic subsystem, which is a primary boundary-spanning component and buffers the input into the coordinative and operating subsystems of the organization.

For any organization to be seen as a system it must have boundaries separating it from its environment. An organization's boundaries are usually vague. Nonetheless, boundaries perform the functions of (1) demarcation between organization and environment; (2) regulation of the flow of information, material, and people into and out of the system; and (3) protection of the system from environmental stresses. An important aspect of boundaries is the degree to which they are receptive to inputs. The boundaries of most human service organizations are easily penetrated, are quite open to external influences, and have many transactions with the environment. [12]

Since information from the environment must pass through the boundaries of the organization before reaching organizational decision makers, managers who represent the organization in its contacts with constituencies outside it perform a key function in boundary spanning as exchange agents between the organization and its task environment.

The nature and extent of the boundary-spanning activities largely determine whether or not the agency adapts to changes in the environment. The boundary spanner is an advocate of change. Bennis considers the boundary spanner responsible for changing attitudes, perceptions, and values of organizational members. [13]

Evidence of the dynamics of the representing function is difficult to ascertain because of the diverse nomenclature given to the function in the literature. Some authorities suggest that representation is a distinct management function. They have in mind the manager who represents his organization in trade associations and government relationships with a view to modifying the external environment or committing the organization to a contractual obligation, or the manager who represents his department in committee meetings which may affect the internal environment. Other authorities do not consider representation to be a separate function because it appears to be a complex consisting of communication and the exercise of authority, directing, coordinating, and organizing. [14]

For our purpose, these ambiguities do not present serious problems, for if we consider representing as a boundary-spanning function, it can be identified whether it is performed as a distinct function or encompassed under other functions.

Schneider's study of behavioral activities for each of nine management functions lists the following under representing:

1. stating the purpose, goals, and objectives of an agency in a public forum
2. writing descriptive materials such as flyers, pamphlets, or brochures about an agency program
3. preparing written news releases for newspapers
4. utilizing audiovisual materials to explain agency programs
5. articulating an agency's role or relationship to other service delivery systems at an interdisciplinary forum
6. recruiting a board member for an agency
7. presenting an agency's budget or programs before its board of trustees
8. analyzing and assessing local public opinion on social services or on particular agency programs
9. developing and evaluating a comprehensive public relations package for a particular agency program. [15]

Patti *et al.*, [16] in another curriculum development study employing the classical approach, list thirteen categories of management functions and classify the following activities under the heading of representing:

1. expressing clearly the purposes, programs, and activities of the organization to outside groups, especially those groups that are uninformed about and/or unsympathetic to the agency's purpose
2. making oral presentations in public forums, both prepared and extemporaneous
3. engaging in public debate
4. utilizing mass media in promoting a positive agency image in the community
5. giving legislative testimony.

These lists are not intended to be exhaustive. They serve only to identify examples of activities in which managers engage when performing certain functions.

Departing from the classical approach of Schneider and Patti *et al.*, Mintzberg [17] has postulated a set of ten roles which encompass the activities of organizational management. These roles are divided into three groupings:

A. Interpersonal roles

    1. figurehead
    2. liaison
    3. leader

B. Informational roles

    1. nerve center
    2. disseminator
    3. spokesman

C. Decisional roles

    1. entrepreneur
    2. disturbance handler
    3. resource allocator
    4. negotiator

Mintzberg presents his roles as an integrated whole whose parts are not easily separable. For our purpose, however, these roles must be separated to allow examination of those activities which advance the interest of the organization through contacts with the environment.

An examination of Mintzberg's roles reveals that the liaison and spokesman roles involve a considerable degree of representing activity. Mintzberg states that "the liaison role is devoted to building up the manager's own external information system — informal, private, verbal, but nevertheless, effective."[18] In this role the manager spends nearly one-third of his time with people outside the organization. He has contacts with an extremely wide range of people: clients, business associates, suppliers, managers of similar organizations, government and trade officials, and committee and board members.[19] In the spokesman role, the manager sends information to people outside his organization. He must inform and satisfy the influential members of the public, consumer groups, and government officials.[20]

It is not the writer's intention to try to functionalize Mintzberg's model but only to identify the activities, functions, or roles which make up that part of the manager's job included in representing. However categorized, these activities, functions, or roles are becoming more and more important to the life of modern organizations. Organizational change is increasingly externally induced and an organization can adapt only if it can learn from and adjust its functioning in accordance with the changes in the environment.

An organization interacts continually with other organizations, individuals, groups, and other constituencies in its environment. Each has some claim on the organization and a set of expectations, and each is affected by different issues in different ways. Managers can no longer ignore what is "outside" their organizations. The last decade has witnessed a growing environmental turbulence, which has created a new appreciation and understanding of environmental forces. Student unrest, minority group protests, the consumer movement, the women's rights movement, and concerns about ecology, the meaning of work, the quality of life, the environment, and "power to the people" will continue to influence profoundly the future of human service organizations. An understanding of environmental forces and change is the key requisite for the management function of representing. This understanding and the input derived from it must be an integral part of all management functions, activities, and roles. Relevant environmental components are critical to all the organization's decision-making processes. "The message to [representing] managers is clear: The values and needs of society must be reflected in the alternatives considered and the priorities assigned to managers"[21].

The process of monitoring the environment encompasses varied information transactions that may fall outside the formally prescribed activities of representing the agency. Activities such as reading magazines and newspapers, receiving governmental or client analysis reports, and compiling reports from available data, as well as interacting (verbally or in writing) with individuals, groups, and constituencies external to the organization, all might be considered activities of the agency representative.[22]

In "advancing the interests of the agency through contacts with individuals, groups, or constituencies outside the organization,"[23] the agency representative is performing an organization/environment exchange activity. Looking closely at the complexity of that relationship, it seems reasonable to expand our view of the representing function to include those activities more appropriately defined as boundary-spanning.

Steiner points out this complexity:

> Human service managers must face the fact that there is a growing chasm between the public and the provider. Hostility is manifested not only in terms of increased verbal dissatisfaction, but also in falling budgetary allocations. Government and public are no longer willing to tolerate vague pronouncements of "do goodism" as substitutes for observable program impacts. They are demanding proof of accomplishments rather than continued promise of future benefits. . . . What many managers fail to realize is that while the public consumes services to satisfy legitimate need, they are also the ultimate controller over how resources are distributed to clients. The public, as clients, demand more and

*more, but as stockholders they want less and less expenditure. The
reality is that not everyone can be pleased.*[24]

Robbins does not help simplify the picture of the agency representative's relationship with the outside population when he states:

*Much of the population has become discouraged by the difficulty of
obtaining open and truthful comments from organizational spokesmen. The environment created in recent years . . . has destroyed
much of the public trust . . . . A public that has been largely
disillusioned by those who have abused its openness and assumed
its gullibility is going to scrutinize even more cautiously the official
statements made by organization [representatives].*[25]

Unfortunately, neither education nor experience has prepared the human
service manager to deal effectively with the current role of representing the
agency as a boundary spanner between the turbulent environment and the
organization.

The descriptions of the roles, functions, and skills of managers in their
representing activities as suggested by Patti *et al.*, Mintzberg, and Schneider
give the impression that managers are insulated from the "hot" issues of
constituencies' pressures. The study by Patti *et al.* indicated that representing was not listed among the five most important functions for more than
seventy percent of the managers studied. However, it was considered more
significant than the time given to it and a disproportionate number of
managers judged it to be among the most significant activities they performed.[26]

A manager usually is accountable to not one but several constituencies
and his relationships with them are important to his success. He must weigh
and balance the often conflicting views and pressures from public and
special interests. He often is accountable to several competing constituencies, who marshall pressures in support of or in opposition to the
agency's program. All the activities of these constituencies are part of the
complex and important environment within which the manager must function.[27]

In his representing function, the manager has the difficult task of
winning recognition, respect, and trust from the agency's constituencies,
gaining their support, and yet retaining his independence and informed,
balanced judgment.

In order to survive, the human service agency is dependent on the legislature for authorization and funds, on the labor market for employees, on the voter for support, on the culture for values and norms, and on the existence of clientele to serve. In order to continue and to grow, the agency must interact successfully with these elements of the environment. It is the function of agency representing — the art of boundary spanning — to establish and maintain that interaction.[28]

In the face of conflicting pressures, competing constituencies, diminishing resources, and a generally turbulent environment, organizations in the future will be increasingly subject to external forces and must be prepared to adapt.

FOOTNOTES

1. E. F. Kast and J. E. Rosenzweig, *Organization and Management* (New York: McGraw-Hill, 1970), p. 4.

2. D. Katz and R. Kahn, *The Social Psychology of Organizations* (New York: John Wiley and Sons, 1966), pp. 14-15.

3. Ibid., pp. 19-26.

4. D. Hellriegel and J. Slocum, *Organizational Behavior: Contingency Views* (St. Paul: West Publishing Co., 1976), pp. 5-7.

5. Ibid.

6. S. P. Robbins, *The Administrative Process* (New York: Prentice-Hall, 1976), pp. 34-36; Kast and Rosenzweig, 1970, pp. 54-56.

7. Kast and Rosenzweig, 1970, p. 135.

8. F. Luthans, *Organization Behavior* (New York: McGraw-Hill, 1977), pp. 53-57.

9. Kast and Rosenzweig, 1970, p. 136.

10. Ibid., p. 138.

11. J. D. Thompson, *Organization in Action* (New York: McGraw-Hill, 1967), pp. 27-28.

12. M. Rosenberg and R. Brody, *Systems Serving People: A Breakthrough in Service Delivery* (Cleveland: Case Western Reserve University, 1974), pp. 11-13.

13. R. Leifer and A. Delbecq, "Organizational/Environmental Interchange: A Model of Boundary Spanning Activity," *Academy of Management Review* (January 1978): 40-48.

14. H. Koontz and C. O'Donnell, *Management: A Systems and Contingency Analysis of Managerial Functions* (New York: McGraw-Hill, 1976), pp. 46-48.

15. R. L. Schneider, "Behavioral Outcome for Administrative Majors," *Journal of Education for Social Work* 14 (Winter 1978): 102-110.

16. R. Patti *et al.*, *Educating for Management in Social Welfare,* Social Welfare Management Curriculum Development Project, University of Washington, Seattle, July 1976.

17. H. Mintzberg, "The Manager's Job: Folklore and Fact," *Harvard Business Review* (July-August 1975): 54-59.

18. Ibid.

19. Ibid.

20. Ibid.

21. J. L. Gibson, J. Ivancevich, and J. Donnelly, *Organizations: Behavior, Structure, Processes* (Dallas: Business Publications, 1976), pp. 7-8.

22. Leifer and Delbecq, 1978.

23. Definition used by the Institute for Human Service Management, 1401 21st Street, Sacramento, California, in the "Guidelines for Authors" developed for the First Annual Conference.

24. R. Steiner, *Managing the Human Services* (Beverly Hills: Sage Publications, 1977), p. 155.

25. Robbins, 1976, p. 154.

26. Patti *et al.*, 1976.

27. J. J. Corso and R. S. Paul, *Men Near The Top* (Baltimore: The Johns Hopkins Press, 1977), pp. 39-41.

28. Steiner, 1977, pp. 157-59.

REFERENCES

Corso, J.J., and Paul, R.S. *Men Near The Top*. Baltimore, Md.: The Johns Hopkins Press, 1977.

Gibson, J.L.; Ivancevich, J.; and Donnelly, J. *Organizations: Behavior, Structure, Processes*. Dallas: Business Publications, 1976.

Hellriegel, D., and Slocum, J. *Organizational Behavior: Contingency Views*. St. Paul, Minn.: West Publishing Co., 1976.

Kast, E.F., and Rosenzweig, J.E. *Organization and Management*. New York: McGraw-Hill, 1970.

Katz, D., and Kahn, R. *The Social Psychology of Organizations*. New York: John Wiley and Sons, 1966.

Koontz, H., and O'Donnell, C. *Management: A Systems and Contingency Analysis of Managerial Functions*. New York: McGraw-Hill, 1976.

Leifer, R., and Delbecq, A. "Organizational/Environmental Interchange: A Model of Boundary-Spanning Activity." *Academy of Management Review* (January 1978): 40-48.

Luthans, F. *Organization Behavior*. New York: McGraw-Hill, 1977.

Mintzberg, H. "The Manager's Job: Folklore and Fact." *Harvard Business Review* (July-August 1975): 54-59.

Patti, R. *et al. Educating for Management in Social Welfare*. Social Welfare Management Curriculum Development Project. University of Washington, Seattle, July 1976.

Robbins, S.P. *The Administrative Process*. New York: Prentice-Hall, 1976.

Rosenberg, M., and Brody, R. *Systems Serving People: A Breakthrough in Service Delivery*. Cleveland: Case Western Reserve University, 1974.

Schneider, R.L. "Behavioral Outcome for Administrative Majors." *Journal of Education for Social Work* 14 (Winter 1978): 102-10.

Steiner, R. *Managing the Human Services*. Beverly Hills: Sage Publications, 1977.

Thompson, J.D. *Organization in Action*. New York: McGraw-Hill, 1967.

USING ECONOMIC INCENTIVES
TO BALANCE BUDGETS

Fred Thompson

Economists frequently argue that many of the services provided by governments and supported by budget allocations should be competitively supplied. Examples of such services include public housing, higher education, and recreational and cultural services. Niskanen has claimed that wherever a service can be effectively marketed to customers, competition ought to be promoted and the public's interest in the augmentation of the supply of the service ought to be expressed by means of a per-unit subsidy.[1]

The justification for this claim rests upon the observation that a set of nonprofit organizations, offering a service at a uniform price in response to a per-unit subsidy and customer demand, will generate an allocatively and technically efficient solution to the service supply problem.[2] In theory, of course, the same solution can be obtained by means of administrative budget controls. However, central administrative controls are costly. Moreover, their costs are overheads: administrative controls contribute nothing to the provision of public goods and services. At best, the efforts of central control agencies, such as the Federal Office of Management and Budget or state departments of finance, can do no more than assure an efficient supply of public services. Economists argue, therefore, that wherever competitive supply can provide this assurance, it should be preferred to direct governmental provision simply because it permits avoidance of direct control costs.

Furthermore, it is frequently suggested that, in the public sector, constraints are imposed on control agencies which guarantee that budgets will contain considerable slack. Politicians generally want to spend as much money as they can, subject to the limits imposed by the requirements of sound fiscal policy and revenue estimates. This attitude results in expectations that actual expenditure must be equal to or less than the budget-authorized amount and that program performance must be equal to or greater than the budget forecast. Since control agencies are held accountable for meeting these expectations, budgeters give high priority to certainty. Unfortunately, as Stedry has observed, budgeted performance levels which can be obtained with a frequency approaching certainty cannot be very ambitious. Indeed, any goal which is designed to be obtainable most of the time is necessarily low.[3]

173

THE PROBLEM

Despite the manifest advantage of competitive supply and per-unit subsidies, public services continue to be provided by monopoly supply with direct administrative controls from central control agencies. If the behavior of a significant number of service suppliers (i.e., all those who can market their services to customers) can be controlled much more efficiently through the management of revenue schedules, why are per-unit subsidies so rare?

One reason frequently given for rejecting the use of market controls is that greater reliance upon per-unit subsidies, together with increased competition, would make budget planning more difficult. This is a plausible explanation. Budgeters highly value certainty. With a per-unit subsidy, the total would be determined by customer demand, predictions of which unfortunately are often unreliable. It would therefore appear that the use of per-unit subsidies would be inconsistent with the control agency's need for certainty about total expenditure and performance levels. Were this explanation valid, one might conclude that the benefits associated with the exploitation of market controls are unobtainable without wholesale changes in the structure of the budget process, changes which seem unlikely to occur.

However, it is not certain that greater reliance upon per-unit subsidies does increase the difficulty of budget planning. Indeed, the identification of per-unit subsidies with budgetary uncertainty appears to ignore a substantial array of financial techniques that could, in theory, greatly reduce or even eliminate the budgeting problem.[4] These techniques include borrowing, nonprice rationing, and especially the use of incentives to induce service providers to predict more accurately the total demand for a service. Failure to recognize these alternatives is hardly surprising, since they are not part of the standard repertoire of public-sector financial management techniques. Even in the private sector, the role of economic incentives in budgetary control systems is only beginning to be appreciated.[5] However, saying a technique is unfamiliar is different from saying it does not exist.

Of course, the existence of theoretical uncertainty-reducing techniques does not guarantee their adoption by central control agencies. What works in theory may not work in practice. Since central control agencies are averse to uncertainty, unless it can be shown that these techniques work in practice it is doubtful that they will be tried. In fact, students of policy diffusion have conclusively demonstrated that governments seldom adopt policy innovations that have not been shown to be effective elsewhere.[6]

THE RUSSIAN SOLUTION

If the issue is that per-unit subsidies may cause budget planning problems, we should look for techniques that have, in practice, successfully overcome these problems. This paper suggests that it might be profitable to look somewhat further afield than is usually done in discussions of public sector financial management problems: to Russia.

The relevance of the Soviet experience with a centrally planned economy to problems of public administration in Western democracies is obvious. However, public administrators typically resist the notion that we might learn from the Russians. In this case this view is clearly wrong, since the Russians have had far more experience with the use of economic incentives in budget control systems than we have.

The use of economic incentives in budgetary control requires a substantial reorientation of the budgeter's role in the budget enforcement process. Demski and Feltham have suggested that a budget is essentially a contract.[7] In the public sector in Western democracies it is a contract between a service provider and the political decision makers which is negotiated and enforced by a central control agency. Enforcement is typically by means of the budgeter's imposition or threat of imposition of sanctions on the service provider if he fails to perform at the level specified in the budget. It is implicitly understood that the budgetary penalties imposed upon the service provider will depend on the kind and source of failure. There is one penalty for under-performance and another for over-performance and a distinction is usually drawn between variances resulting from uncontrollable changes in the service provider's environment and those resulting from managerial failure.[8]

The incentive approach, on the other hand, requires that a budget be designed in such a way that the service provider will find the terms offered by the central control agency the most attractive option available to him.[9] The problem is to design per-unit subsidies which will induce the service provider to place a high premium on the accuracy of his performance or output estimate.

The Soviet solution to this problem arose from a genuine need to have producers reveal their output level ahead of time.[10] As Weitzman[11] has noted:

> *The primary reason for planning is the need for coordination. In order to have tightly coordinated plans, it really is indispensable to*

know (at least approximately) who will be producing what. This is especially crucial for intermediate goods, where too little can be a disaster, and too much is practically worthless.

In such a situation, the use of targets or quotas is unavoidable. At the same time, the planners (the central control agents in the Soviet system) must overcome "the built-in tendency for managers to underrepresent their potential in seeking low assignments."[12] The Russian solution is to make the manager's bonus depend on the plan's target.

The Soviet incentive system includes the following phases. First, the planners issue planning estimates on the basis of their current knowledge. These estimates include both an output target level and a tentative bonus fund. Second, the manager is given the option of selecting a higher or lower planned output level with a higher or lower planned bonus for meeting it, according to the following formula:

$$B_2 = B_1 + \beta (y_2 - y_1)$$

where B_1 = the planners' tentative bonus fund
B_2 = the manager's proposed bonus fund
y_1 = the planners' initial output target level
y_2 = the manager's proposed output level
β = a coefficient representing the per-unit bonus for output increments.

In the third, or plan implementation, phase, the manager produces an output and receives a bonus based on the following formula if he exceeds his proposed output level:

$$B_3 = B_2 + \alpha(y_3 - y_2)$$

where B_3 = the actual bonus
y_3 = the actual output level
α = a coefficient representing the per-unit bonus for output increments over the proposed output level.

and on the following formula if he fails to achieve his proposed output level:

$$B_3 = B_2 + \gamma(y_3 - y_2)$$

where γ = a coefficient representing the per-unit bonus for output decrements under the proposed output level.

Obviously, under this system, if the manager knows what he can produce and if γ is greater than β and β is greater than α he will set his proposed output at that level, since in this way he will always obtain the maximum possible bonus.

Furthermore, Weitzman has demonstrated that under uncertainty:

> *By raising α lowering β or raising γ the planners can induce more conservative (lower) plan targets — which are more likely to be fulfilled. By doing the opposite they can stimulate more ambitious targets.* [13]

Weitzman has noted that, in any case, output level should not be treated as a wholly random variable, since

> *. . . in reality effort can also influence output. With extra effort an enterprise may be able to increase its production possibilities. The effect is to stabilize realized output closer to the announced target level. This helps to make the output quota a more meaningful concept to the planners because they can count on it more.* [14]

The relationship of this scheme to our budget process is clear. The first phase corresponds to the planning estimates phase, the second to budget negotiation, and the third to budget implementation. We need only redefine the variables in the Soviet incentive scheme to adapt it to our budget planning problem. That is:

B_1 = the central control agency's base line budget estimate
y_1 = the central control agency's base line output level estimate
B_2 = the service provider's proposed budget
y_2 = the service provider's proposed output level
B_3 = the service provider's actual budget
y_3 = the service provider's actual output level

and

β = a coefficient representing the per-unit subsidy for output increments

α = a coefficient representing the per-unit subsidy for output increments above the service provider's proposed output level

γ = a coefficient representing the per-unit subsidy (penalty) for output decrements below the service provider's proposed output level.

To apply Weitzman's conclusions about the effects of the Soviet incentive scheme to the budget planning problem, we need only assume that service providers will try to get as big a budget as possible and that they will spend everything they get.[15]

SOME CONCLUDING OBSERVATIONS

The significance of the Soviet incentive system is that it is in use and apparently works. Experimentation by public administrators (especially central controllers) with structurally similar mechanisms seems justified. However, care should be taken to select programs which presently receive public support based on measurable performance and agreed-upon output measures. Furthermore, it might be appropriate to seek out services which, for one reason or another, have resisted the application of direct administrative controls. These suggestions follow from the assumption that innovations are more likely to be accepted if they are seen as incremental modifications of existing practices.

At the state level, an appropriate candidate for experimentation might be higher education services. In the first place, institutional budget allocations are usually based upon measurable performance targets expressed in terms of enrollments. In the second place, the tradition (and in some cases legal requirement) of institutional autonomy has frequently confounded attempts to apply direct managerial controls in higher education. The explicit use of per-student subsidies therefore ought to be perceived as a minor change in control practices. In the third place, in higher education (unlike many public services) the supply of services is not monopolized by one or a few providers. Most regions contain a number of more or less competing institutions. Finally, most of the intergovernmental coordination problems that are encountered in the supply of a substantial number of public services are absent in this case. Since higher education policy and support are largely state responsibilities, changes in control practices would not require the approval of higher or lower level jurisdictions.

The point is that the problems that will be encountered in attempting to implement the use of incentives in budget control systems should be minimized by starting in a field such as higher education, where application should be easy. Further exploration of this issue undoubtedly will uncover other suitable candidates for experimentation. At the same time it should be understood that the direct benefits derived from easy applications are likely to be small. Vindication of a program of budgetary incentives may not be obtained from the direct benefits of a few pilot projects.

The indirect benefits of such projects are of greater importance. Successful employment of per-unit subsidies by central control agencies should reduce the uncertainty associated with their use. Experience should provide budgeters with confidence in their ability to design incentive mechanisms that reflect not only the purposes of the provision of public services but also the need to satisfy organizational and political concerns. The vindication of the use of per-unit subsidies is to be sought, therefore, in the incorporation of a range of incentive mechanisms in the standard repertoire of control practices employed by budgeters.

FOOTNOTES

1. W. A. Niskanen, Jr., *Bureaucracy and Representative Government* (Chicago and New York: Aldine-Atherton, 1971), p. 105.

2. Ibid.

3. A. C. Stedry, "Budgetary Control: A Behavioral Approach," Sloan School of Management, Working Paper 43-64. Stedry describes a laboratory situation in which it was found that budgets which were good predictors of performance produced lower performance levels than budgets with performance targets high enough that they were obtained only half the time.

4. Niskanen, 1971, p. 105.

5. See J. S. Demski and G. A. Feltham, "Economic Incentives in Budget Control Systems," *Accounting Review* (April 1978), and *Cost Determination: A Conceptual Approach* (Ames, Iowa: Iowa State University Press, 1976). See also T. Kobyashi, "Structure of Incentives and Mechanisms for Collective Decision Making," Unpublished Paper, Department of Economics, Stanford University, February 1977; and L.S. Fan, "On the Reward System," *American Economic Review* 65 (March 1975): 226-29.

6. R. Eyestone, "Confusion, Diffusion, and Innovation," *American Political Science Review* 71 (June 1977): 441-47.

7. Demski and Feltham, 1978.

8. It should be noted that, even though this is the standard approach to budget enforcement in the public sector (an approach that might loosely be described as management by exception), the techniques of control employed are quite unsophisticated. The reader might contrast existing control techniques in the public sector with those described in a good "state of the art" textbook on managerial accounting, such as C. T. Horngren, *Cost Accounting: A Managerial Emphasis* (Englewood Cliffs, N.J.: Prentice-Hall, 1972). See also R. N. Anthony and R. Herzlinger, *Management Control in Non-Profit Organizations* (Homewood, Ill.: Richard D. Irwin, Inc., 1975); and C. T. Horngren, "Accounting Principles: Private or Public Sector?" *Journal of Accountancy* (May 1972a).

9. Demski and Feltham, 1978.

10. This and the following discussion are based upon M. L. Weitzman, "The New Soviet Incentive Model," *The Bell Journal of Economics* 7 (Spring 1976): 251-57. See also J. S. Berliner, *Innovation in Soviet Industry,* Chapter 14, "General Incentives and Decision Rules" (Cambridge, Mass.: M.I.T. Press, 1975); M. Ellman, "Bonus Formulae and Soviet Managerial Performance: A Further Comment," *Southern Economic Journal* (April 1973): 652-53; and W. A. Leeman, "Bonus Formulae and Soviet Managerial Performance," *Southern Economic Review* (April 1970): 434-45.

11. Weitzman, 1976, pp. 252-53.

12. Ibid.

13. Ibid., p. 255.

14. Ibid. For Weitzman's demonstration of the logic of this assertion, see pp. 255-56.

15. See J. L. Zimmerman, "Budget Uncertainty and the Allocation Decision in a Nonprofit Organization," *Journal of Accounting Research* (Autumn 1976).

REFERENCES

Anthony, R.N., and Herzlinger, R. *Management Control in Non-Profit Organizations*. Homewood, Ill.: Richard D. Irwin, Inc., 1975.

Berliner, J.S. *Innovation in Soviet Industry*. Cambridge, Mass.: M.I.T. Press, 1975.

Demski, J.S., and Feltham, G.A. "Economic Incentives in Budget Control Systems." *Accounting Review* (April 1978).

Demski, J.S., and Feltham, G.A. *Cost Determination: A Conceptual Approach*. Ames, Iowa: Iowa State University Press, 1976.

Ellman, M. "Bonus Formulae and Soviet Managerial Performance: A Further Comment." *Southern Economic Journal* (April 1973): 652-53.

Eyestone, R. "Confusion, Diffusion, and Innovation." *American Political Science Review* 71 (June 1977): 441-47.

Fan, L.S. "On the Reward System." *American Economic Review* 65 (March 1975): 226-29.

Horngren, C.T. *Cost Accounting: A Managerial Emphasis*. Englewood Cliffs, N.J.: Prentice-Hall, 1972.

Horngren, C.T. "Accounting Principles: Private or Public Sector?" *Journal of Accountancy* (May 1972).

Kobyashi, T. "Structure of Incentives and Mechanisms for Collective Decision Making." Unpublished Paper. Department of Economics, Stanford University, February 1977.

Leeman, W.A. "Bonus Formulae and Soviet Managerial Performance." *Southern Economic Review* (April 1970): 434-45.

Niskanen, W. A., Jr. *Bureaucracy and Representative Government*. Chicago and New York: Aldine-Atherton, 1971.

Stedry, A. C. "Budgetary Control: A Behavioral Approach." Sloan School of Management, Working Paper 43-64.

Weitzman, M. L. "The New Soviet Incentive Model." *The Bell Journal of Economics* 7 (Spring 1976): 251-57.

Zimmerman, J. L. "Budget Uncertainty and the Allocation Decision in a Nonprofit Organization." *Journal of Accounting Research* (Autumn 1976).

BUDGET MANAGEMENT IN
THE HUMAN SERVICES

Mitchel J. Lazarus

Although I have some knowledge of and interest in the theory of the budget process, my primary qualifications in the area of human service agency budgeting come from having been a worker in several voluntary agencies; the director of a settlement house and two Jewish Community Centers; and, for the past several years, the Director of Planning and Budgeting for the Minneapolis Federation for Jewish Service. Because of this practical involvement, and because I review small and intermediate agency budgets totalling from $100,000 to $1,000,000, I will focus primarily on budget management for operations of this size. Having established my focus, I want to make the following points:

1. *Budgeting is but one part of an administrative management system.* Budgeting is only one part of the continuum of administration. Human service agency management includes the establishment and review of the agency's mission and goals; the planning of activities and programs to meet goals; the identification of clients to be served and the outreach to them; the securing and mobilization of personnel, facilities, supplies, materials, and dollar resources (including preparation and presentation of a budget); budget management; staff training, deployment, and supervision; the establishment and use of data systems for service evaluation; the securing and education of a sponsoring constituency; and so on. A discussion of budgeting, therefore, while instructive, is necessarily narrow. One must always remember that budgeting is but one phase of management.

2. *A budget is the agency's financial program plan for a projected time frame.* The budget represents in monetary terms the organization's operating plans for a reasonably foreseeable time period. Although this period is usually a year, some agencies are now budgeting for two-year periods.

In my view, the advantages of saving preparation and presentation time may be more than offset by the increased time lag between preparation time (usually four to six months before the budget becomes effective) and the end of the budget period. The many variables in client population groups and their needs, as well as staff changes, can lead to instabilities that make budget management very difficult for time periods of more than twelve months.

If it is necessary to manage a budget for a longer time period, increased vigilance is needed in monitoring experiences, and a way must be found to make the budget flexible in case expenditure requirements change relative to resources.

3. *The budget is also a tool for providing vital information for unit cost analysis, program accountability, and evaluation, and should be prepared as well as reported on both a line and a program basis.* Line items include memberships, tuitions, sales, and grants; personnel costs, retirement and social security, travel, supplies, telephone, organization dues, etc. Program items reflect the assignment of the line income and expenditure items to the various program or service categories.

If program analysis is to provide meaningful data for cost accounting, for interpretation, for research and evaluation, and for effecting changes in the various services, the program categories selected should be manageable units that are related administratively. The selection of appropriate program categories is a very important task requiring considerable skill. The factors to be considered and the use to which such categories are put merit a separate discussion. However, it can be said here that the selection should relate to the easily identified major program areas into which an agency's clients and staff fall.

Once programs or services have been selected, they should be further divided into descriptive units that can be counted or measured, permitting program costs to be assigned to service outcomes. For example, in a family service agency with which I am familiar the programs are divided into eight service categories, as follows:

— Individual and family counseling
— Preventive and enrichment service
— Vocational service
— Resettlement service
— Group counseling
— Services to the aged
— Volunteer service
— Poverty program

While service statistics are expressed as the number of families or persons served, cost units are expressed as the number of interviews or group sessions attended; hence the cost is stated as per interview or group session. The major factor monitored for assigning costs is workers' time. Workers are therefore required to maintain a record of time spent in each of the designated program areas and of the number of interviews or groups conducted. Since an agency's services change, the program divisions and units to be counted or measured must be reviewed and possibly changed from time to time.

While cost accounting is used for interpretation, research, and evaluation, the preparation, management, and updating of a program budget system is another level of budget management in the context of an administrator's total responsibility.

4. *Initial budgets must be recast as working budgets.* Once allocations or grants are made, the initial budget must be revised to reflect known income resources and whatever changes (in population groups, personnel, etc.) may have occurred between the time the budget was prepared and the time it takes effect.

The complexity of budget recasting will depend on the size of the organization and the severity of the allocation reductions. If the changes will affect programs (as they usually do), line and department staff as well as lay boards should be involved. Revising a budget should be part of the participant management style of most agencies.

5. *The budget is a tool for monitoring the agency's financial condition.* To be used in monitoring the agency's financial condition, a budget must be divided into meaningful time periods (usually monthly segments) for obtaining regular financial statements to keep track of income and expense.

The reports must be provided regularly, as soon as possible after the end of the time period selected. A lengthy delay between the end of the time period and the report provides a ''time lag,'' when control can be lost.

The bookkeeping system and the reports should be established and maintained by qualified accountants, not by untrained clerical staff or social workers. Most agencies have unique services, or variations in sources or flow of income and expenditure, requiring special system adaptations and reports.

More agencies should consider adopting an accrual rather than a cash system, so that they know their financial status more accurately. In my view, the result is worth the extra work involved.

6. *Some comments on the nature of financial reports*. Financial reports also should be presented on both a line and a program basis.

The reports should include, at a minimum, the following data:

— the twelve-month working budget
— the month's experience being reported
— the cumulative experience to date
— the balance remaining in the fiscal year.

If the agency has a fairly uniform monthly income and monthly expense, a simple pro rata statement of the proportion of income and expense which should be expected at the end of each month and each cumulative time period also can be provided for comparison with the results.

If, however (as is often the case), the agency has fluctuating but repetitive income and expenditure, better control can be achieved by showing also the experiences of the previous year for the same month or time period and for the cumulative to date. These experiences can be expressed as percentages of the previous year's totals and the percentages can be applied to this year's budgets to make projections.

If the agency will have unique fluctuations for a given year, or allocations for specified programs, the previous year's experience can be used as a guide only for selected categories of income and expense. The agency will then need the assistance of a better than average accountant to chart the flow and rate of variable income in relation to expenditure and to maintain separate ledgers and reports for the allocation designated for each program. This situation can become very complex and requires unique system controls, particularly in large organizations with varied programs and funding sources.

7. *Monthly reports, when added together and closely monitored and understood, are the tools for budget reviews, control, and change*. Major reviews should be held at least quarterly, with staff responsible for department budget expenditure discussing where changes can or should be made. If the organization has a structure involving lay persons or public officials in a policy or advisory role, they should participate also in the review process, usually after the executive and staff have reviewed the total agency budget and have recommendations to make. In some agencies, the lay committees, guided by the staff, make the final decisions on changes.

8. *The procedures of budget control for the agency as a whole apply equally to the fiscal control of departments*. Monthly or other timely reports

must be provided to the workers in charge of a program area if fiscal accountability is to be expected. Even more important, the workers responsible for a program must learn to read and use the reports if they are to know where their department stands fiscally. Within guidelines already established, or in consultation with a supervisor or executive, a department head can make adjustments as needed to maintain control and accountability.

9. *Sound fiscal management is also required for and linked with the continuing program review and evaluation expected of human service agencies.* Whether or not its funding bodies require zero-based budgeting, an agency should engage in an ongoing process of program review leading to discontinuation, reduction, modification, or expansion of existing programs and/or the addition of new programs.

While, ideally, this process would call for simultaneous in-depth review of all major programs, such a comprehensive review within a short time span is usually not feasible. The agency should therefore select each year one or several programs for a thorough and basic review.

In this program review process, gross costs for program packages and unit costs per output are very important data. Even without the more elusive objective research data on program effectiveness, accurate program costs are important measuring tools in the evaluation process. The subjective judgment of professional staff on the effectiveness of the services provided is supported or tempered by cost data.

10. *Finally, fiscal management skills needed will vary with the size and complexity of the agency.* The directors of small or intermediate service agencies, or of small or intermediate departments, do not need to master complex skills. Although an ability to read and understand financial statements is necessary, this can be acquired easily from supervisors and/or accountants. A willingness to spend time in reviewing such statements in detail and to ask questions of colleagues is essential. One must also be prepared to take corrective measures within a reasonable period of time.

However, the knowledge, skill, and amount of time required for budget management increases with budget size, with the variety of services offered, and with the number of sources of funding. Administrative assistants, accountants, and comptrollers are needed in the larger and more complex agencies to assist an executive or department head with budget control. However, even in these larger agencies, administrators must be able to understand and use the budget as a tool within the broad context of management.

PART 3

EVALUATING RESULTS IN THE HUMAN SERVICES

Evaluation often has been overlooked or ignored in human service management. As indicated earlier, this neglect has resulted in part from the concern of human service professionals for process. In addition, there are many difficulties associated with the performance of evaluations in the human services. For any business there is a financial bottom line which is not obscured by values or attitudes and which provides easy access to information about the success of the organization. Similarly, any business is concerned about the quality, durability, and investment return of its product. The measurement of these factors gives straightforward information on the impact, efficiency, and overall effectiveness of the particular product.

For the human service program, a look at the financial bottom line may provide little important information on the worth of a particular product or of the organization which produces it. In addition, questions of quality, durability, and ultimate return on resources invested often must be answered with approximations rather than direct information. Information necessary to evaluate the outcome, effectiveness, and efficiency of, for example, a mental health program would involve extensive assessments rather than a few critical dimensions.

In this section of the book, some of the major concerns in the evaluation of human service organizations are considered. Three questions must be faced in reviewing human service programs. The first is the question of *how well*? Answering this question involves the consideration of issues of goal attainment and efficiency. Specifically, programs must be reviewed by assessing the degree to which goals are met and the costs associated with achieving these goals.

A second major evaluation question is *so what*? The concern here is with the impact of a program on solving or reducing the problem it addresses. A well-run, cost-efficient program does not necessarily contribute to the solution of a major social problem.

A final question addressed in this section is *what if*? This question focuses on the search for alternatives. A constant exploration of new approaches is critical to improvement in the human services.

Macht and Seidl provide practical guidelines on the use of evaluation to increase the effectiveness of a human service program. By identifying key organizational variables, the authors help the manager to determine what type of evaluation is suited to a program's needs at different stages in its development. The authors warn that evaluation can lead to premature termination of innovative programs.

Washington discusses the need for social workers to be able to assess the effectiveness of their interventions under specific conditions. He states that if measurements of effectiveness are standardized, differences in outcome are more likely than at present to be related to differences in intervention. He considers some of the evaluation problems which are particular to the human services.

Describing the basic steps in the evaluation process and providing a practical example of their application, D'Agostino suggests that evaluation can be used as a tool for assessing both proposals and programs. He views program evaluation as a natural extension of a proposal's evaluation plan.

Using as his example the experiences of the California State Department of Social Services, Dawson suggests criteria and measures for evaluating performance in a cash grant welfare system. He presents a three-dimensional performance model for comparing governmental units. With the use of this model, the source and extent of management problems become apparent and resources can be concentrated on the solution of critical problems.

A CONTINGENCY APPROACH
TO EVALUATION:
MANAGERS' GUIDELINES

Fredrick W. Seidl
Mary W. Macht

In the 1970s, evaluation has become an increasingly important issue for human service administrators. Two basic concerns have been whether service interventions are effective and how evaluation research can help management improve program performance. The purpose of this paper is to provide practical guidelines to human service administrators on the use of evaluation research to increase the effectiveness of human service programs.

Instead of presenting a model for solving specific evaluation problems, we are presenting a guide to the analysis of organizational variables important to evaluation research. The basic strategy suggested is to identify key variables which can guide managers in determining the types of evaluation which will produce the knowledge needed at the various stages of program development. While ours is not a comprehensive list of organizational variables, each variable is hypothesized to be important in determining who should evaluate, what the reasons for evaluation are, and what form the evaluation should take. The variables discussed are technology, environment, domain, and goals.

TECHNOLOGY

Technology is operationally defined as the mechanism by which organizations produce their service or product. Technology may be seen on a continuum varying along the dimensions of task difficulty and task variability: routine technologies are relatively low on task difficulty and variability, while complex technologies are high on both. As tasks become more complex, it becomes harder to make definite cause and effect statements. This problem has two major implications for evaluation. First, it enhances the ability of program staff to discredit the evaluation. Professionals may argue that either the wrong variables were measured or the right variables were measured in the wrong way. The complexity of the technology increases the probability that their objections are legitimate. Second, people working under conditions of complexity must deal with the uncertainty of cause and effect relationships. They therefore tend to rely heavily on their personal values and ideologies.

While some human service programs involve mainly routine technology, most are established to deal with very complex social problems to which solutions are unknown. We suggest that the greater the task difficulty and task variability the greater the evaluator's need for substantive knowledge of the technology. Under conditions of simple technology, a competent evaluation technician will suffice. Under conditions of complex technology, the evaluator should have: (1) a substantive knowledge of the different operational frameworks used by professionals; (2) a high degree of evaluation sophistication; and (3) a great amount of influence based on professional competence.

Since professionals involved in complex technologies tend to be highly educated and to possess considerable status and power, the evaluator needs to be seen to possess the same traits. Professionals have become accustomed to defining their own success, and definitions of success or failure from lower status researchers are not likely to have much impact.

PROGRAM STAGE AND ENVIRONMENT

The primary diagnostic variable involved in determining the appropriate type of evaluation is the stage of development of the program. In their desire to demonstrate the effectiveness of a program, many administrators have made the mistake of rushing into "experimental design" types of evaluation before the program principles are actually operating.

Social action programs go through three stages of development: initiation, contact, and implementation. In Stage 1 (initiation), the goal of the program is to procure the necessary material, social, and technological resources. In Stage 2 (contact, or client procurement), the goal is to contact potential beneficiaries. In Stage 3 (implementation), the program fully engages its clientele and delivers its service or applies its change technology. To move the program effectively into the implementation stage, allowing services to be delivered with a minimal reversion back to Stages 1 and 2, it is important to connect the appropriate form of evaluation with the appropriate stage of the program.

Dividing social program development into three stages emphasizes the importance of the environment to the functioning of human service organizations. Environment is the totality of the physical and social factors which individuals within an organization take into consideration in decision making. An organization must attempt to create a supportive environment which will allow the technical core to produce its service or product without interference. Each of the program stages has different needs which must be recognized. The requirements of Stage 1 (initiation) and Stage 2 (contact, or client procurement) must continue to be met in Stage 3 (implementation) if the technical core is to be buffered from the environment.

By looking at the environment in terms of attitudes toward the program and stability of environmental support, it is possible to indicate at what stage the program is likely to be functioning and where organizational energies need to be expended (see Figure 1). Specifically, it is proposed that programs in Cell 1, where the environment is benign and stable, have the freedom to concentrate on the implementation stage. As long as the environment remains stable, technologists can focus on improving their technical skill. With these programs, therefore, evaluation should be related to improved performance.

Stability of Environmental Support

	Stable	Dynamic
Benign (high receptivity)	I	II
Hostile (high rejection)	III	IV

Attitude toward program

FIGURE 1
Conception of Environmental Components
(after Thompson, 1967)

Programs in Cell II, where the environment is benign and dynamic, will be likely to move back and forth between the needs of Stages 1 and 3. As long as the environment sees the program as worthwhile, client procurement (Stage 2) should not present a problem. To increase impact under these contingencies, the goals of evaluation should be to improve technology and stabilize the environment. Ideally, improvements in technology should decrease environmental threat.

Programs in Cell III, where the environment is hostile and stable, will continue to have the problems of Stages 2 and 3. Evaluation should focus on problems of client contact and on the improvement of technology.

Under the conditions in Cell IV, where the environment is hostile and dynamic, it is unlikely that the program will move past Stage 1. Administrators must realize that unless they are willing to invest evaluation resources in providing feedback on how to achieve the goals of Stages 1 and 2, evaluation will not be of much value. The stated goals of the program are unlikely to be met when staff members are preoccupied with survival problems. We do not say that under these conditions evaluation should not be done but only that attempts at outcome evaluation may be inappropriate and potentially dysfunctional.

DOMAIN

The domain problem is crucial to human service programs, since the definition of a program's domain indicates what part of the environment must be considered in decision making. Domain consensus defines a set of expectations both for members of an organization and for those with whom they interact in determining what the organization will and will not do. The attainment of a viable domain is a political problem. Evaluation may be needed to help the organization discover what it does best and how it can improve its technology to obtain a unique domain. This evaluation process is especially important for small programs: since they cannot compete with large organizations in many areas, they need to declare a domain which is uniquely theirs.

GOALS

Goals are desired states. A distinctive problem of human service program goals is that they frequently contain ambiguities, inconsistencies, and conflicts. A conflict between the organization's and the evaluator's definitions of success may lead the evaluator to view a program as a failure. Clients too have definitions of success, which may be at variance with those of both the evaluator and the organization.

A schematic by Thompson[1] for viewing two dimensions of goals (ends and means) provides some clues for evaluation (see Figure 2). In evaluating programs in Cell I (complete agreement on ends and means), evaluation can most profitably focus on maximizing the potential of the organization. Findings can be stated in terms of efficiency — i.e., which approach yields the greatest per-unit change, not which is the cheapest. Under such conditions, an experimental design with summative feedback would be most appropriate.

Knowledge of Cause-Effect Relationship

	Known	Unknown
Crystallized	I	II
Ambiguous	III	IV

Nature of goal stages

FIGURE 2
Representation of Thompson's Goal Schematic

In Cell II, where the goals are clear but the means of achieving them are unclear, formative evaluation is called for.[2] Under ideal circumstances, several solutions will be attempted with multiple measures to ensure that participants in each group experience some success. This procedure will reduce resistance when participants are asked to adopt principles that have been successful in another sub-unit. Since cause and effect relationships are not clear, differences in value structures are of concern. In this cell, negotiation and experimentation are more important than the technical excellence of the research design. The use of a classical experimental design with a single dependent variable may exclude important and useful information and make the evaluation irrelevant to the program.

In Cell III, where the goals are ambiguous and cause and effect relationships are known, the importance of the program is in question. In this cell, the type of evaluation that is likely to have the most program value is market research, which will provide data to indicate whether the problem being attacked is important and whether it is affecting a significant number of people. Techniques may include needs assessments, public hearings, a search of the literature, or survey research. Summative evaluation is inappropriate since the goal to be measured is unclear. Formative evaluation is unnecessary since the cause and effect relationship is already known. To summarize, in this cell the program is known to be effective but needs to be sold to the decision makers. Evaluation should address this need.

The fourth cell presents numerous difficulties. If the problem being addressed is insignificant and the program is operating without knowledge of cause and effect, the program should be allowed to end. However, if the problem is important, evaluation can be used to increase the recognition of its importance as well as to increase knowledge of how to deal with it. All of the techniques involved in Cells II and III should be employed. Unfortunately, most human service programs fit within this cell: for our complex social problems we attempt inadequate treatment. Managers and evaluators must realize that in this situation the importance of the problem, not the ineffectiveness of treatment, must be stressed. An authoritative experimental outcome of no effect is likely to immobilize management, leaving unresolved the problem which the program was designed to address.

SUMMARY

The variables presented can now be combined to present propositions or guidelines for evaluation. These propositions will suggest who should evaluate, what should be evaluated, and how evaluation should be executed. There are four major propositions, each with related corollaries concerning the maximizing of evaluative impact.

Proposition 1: *If the program is operating in a benign, stable environment with domain consensus, program effort will be concentrated in the implementation (service delivery) stage.*

Corollary 1a: Given these conditions, if goals are crystallized and technology is routine, then the impact of evaluation will be increased if the methodology is summative evaluation and if the findings are addressed to the professional staff. Substantive knowledge of the technology is not required of the evaluator.

Corollary 1b: Given these conditions, if goals are crystallized and technology is complex, then the impact of the evaluation will be increased if the methodology is formative evaluation, if the findings are addressed to the professional staff, and if the evaluator has substantive knowledge of the technology.

Corollary 1c: Given these conditions, if goals are ambiguous and technology is routine, then the impact of the evaluation will be increased if the methodology is summative evaluation and if the findings are addressed to the administrative and the professional staffs. Substantive knowledge of the technology is not required of the evaluator.

Corollary 1d: Given these conditions, if goals are ambiguous and technology is complex, then the impact of the evaluation will be increased if the methodology is formative evaluation, if the findings are addressed to the administrative and the professional staffs and if the evaluator has substantive knowledge of the technology.

Proposition 2: *If the program is operating in a hostile but stable environment lacking domain consensus, program effort will vacillate between Stage 2 (client recruitment) and Stage 3 (service delivery).*

Corollary 2a: Given these conditions, if goals are crystallized and technology is routine, then the impact of evaluation will be increased if the methodology is summative evaluation and if the findings are addressed to the administrative staff. Substantive knowledge of the technology is not required of the evaluator.

Corollary 2b: Given these conditions, if goals are crystallized and technology is complex, then the impact of evaluation will be increased if the methodology includes both market research and formative evaluation, if the findings are addressed to the administrative and the professional staffs, and if the evaluator has substantive knowledge of the technology.

Corollary 2c: Given these conditions, if goals are ambiguous and technology is routine, then the impact of evaluation will be increased if the methodology includes both market research and summative evaluation and if the findings are addressed to the administrative and the professional staffs. Substantive knowledge of the technology is not required of the evaluator.

Corollary 2d: Given these conditions, if goals are ambiguous and technology is complex, then the impact of evaluation will be increased if the methodology includes both market research and formative evaluation, if the findings are addressed to the administrative staff and to program funders, and if the evaluator has substantive knowledge of the technology.

Proposition 3: *If the program is operating in a benign, dynamic environment with domain consensus, program efforts will vacillate between Stage 1 (obtaining resources) and Stage 3 (service delivery).*

Corollary 3a: Given these conditions, if goals are crystallized and technology is routine, then the impact of evaluation will be increased if the methodology is summative evaluation and if the findings are addressed to the administrative staff. Substantive knowledge of the technology is not required of the evaluator.

Corollary 3b: Given these conditions, if goals are crystallized and technology is complex, then the impact of evaluation will be increased if the methodology is formative evaluation, if the findings are addressed to the administrative and the professional staffs, and if the evaluator has substantive knowledge of the technology.

Corollary 3c: Given these conditions, if goals are ambiguous and technology is routine, then the impact of evaluation will be increased if the methodology is summative evaluation and if the findings are addressed to the administrative staff and to program funders. Substantive knowledge of the technology is not required of the evaluator.

Corollary 3d: Given these conditions, if goals are ambiguous and technology is complex, then the impact of evaluation will be increased if the methodology is formative evaluation, if the findings are addressed to the administrative and the professional staffs as well as to program funders, and if the evaluator has substantive knowledge of the technology.

Proposition 4: *If the program is operating in a hostile, dynamic environment lacking in domain consensus, program efforts will vacillate between Stage 1 (obtaining resources) and Stage 2 (client recruitment).*

Corollary 4a: Given these conditions, if goals are crystallized and technology is routine, then the impact of evaluation will be increased if the methodology includes both market research and summative evaluation and if the findings are addressed to the administrative staff and to program funders. Substantive knowledge of the technology is not required of the evaluator.

Corollary 4b: Given these conditions, if goals are crystallized and technology is complex, then the impact of evaluation will be increased if the methodology includes both market research and formative evaluation, if the findings are addressed to the administrative and the professional staffs as well as to program funders, and if the evaluator has substantive knowledge of the technology.

Corollary 4c: Given these conditions, if goals are ambiguous and technology is routine, then the impact of evaluation will be increased if the methodology includes both market research and formative evaluation and if the findings are addressed to the administrative and the professional staffs as well as to program funders. Substantive knowledge of the technology is not required of the evaluator.

Corollary 4d: Given these conditions, if goals are ambiguous and technology is complex, then the impact of evaluation will be increased if the methodology includes market research and formative evaluation, if the findings are addressed to the administrative and the professional staffs as well as to program funders, and if the evaluator has substantive knowledge of the technology.

DISCUSSION

In this age of accountability, there are two major forces that may cause the premature termination of innovative programs: a tight economy and evaluation research. While fiscal conditions will always be the primary determinant of the resources invested in human services, both managers and evaluators must ensure that in their eagerness to be accountable and scientific they do not terminate worthwhile service programs before they are functioning properly. "No effect" findings have provided not only a healthy skepticism to service providers but also an unhealthy excuse for policy makers to do nothing about social problems because nothing works anyway.

This paper suggests guidelines for human service administrators on the use of evaluation to develop and improve programs. It illustrates the importance of organizational variables as determinants of program success. One of the greatest flaws in evaluation research has been that researchers have tested human service programs without realizing that environmental constraints may not be allowing the programs to happen. Managers can no longer permit summative experimental design evaluation to take place until the program principles being tested are in operation. They must take a proactive stance on what evaluation can provide for program improvement.

FOOTNOTES

1. James Thompson, *Organizations in Action* (New York: McGraw-Hill, 1967).

2. Formative evaluation is concerned with the examination of process and to the extent that one considers the outcomes of the project, one is restricted to looking at progress toward determining goals. Summative evaluation is defined as evaluation design capable of leading to inferences about program worth. See Michael Scriven, "The Methodology of Evaluation," in *Perspectives of Current Evaluation* (AERA Monograph Series on Methodology, Chicago: Rand McNally, 1967).

REFERENCES

Aguilar, Frances. *Scanning the Business Environment.* New York: Macmillan, 1967.

Corwin, Ronald. "Strategies for Organizational Survival." *Journal of Applied Behavioral Science* 8 (1972).

Etzioni, Amitai. *Modern Organizations.* Englewood Cliffs: Prentice-Hall, 1964.

Franklin, Jack, and Thrasher, Jean. *An Introduction to Program Evaluation.* New York: Wiley, 1976.

Freeman, Howard, and Sherwood, Clarence. "Research in Large Scale Intervention Programs." *Journal of Social Issues* 21 (1965): 11-28.

Greenwood, Ernest. "Social Work and Social Science: A Theory of Their Relationship." *Social Service Review* 29 (1955): 24.

Hall, Richard. *Organizations: Structure and Process.* Englewood Cliffs: Prentice-Hall, 1972.

Harvey, Edward. "Technology and the Structure of Organization." *American Sociological Review* 33 (1968): 247-59.

Hasenfeld, Yeshekel, and English, Richard. *Human Service Organizations.* Ann Arbor: University of Michigan Press, 1974.

Kivens, Lawrence, and Bolin, David. "Evaluation in a Community Mental Health Center." *Evaluation* 3 (1976): 98-105.

Lawrence, Paul, and Lorsch, Jay. "Differentiation and Integration in Complex Organizations." *Administrative Science Quarterly* 12 (1967): 1-47.

Perrow, Charles. *Organizational Analysis: A Sociological View.* Belmont, California: Wadsworth, 1970.

Perrow, Charles. "The Analysis of Goals in Complex Organizations." *American Sociological Review* 26 (1961): 856-66.

Salasin, Susan. "Experimentation Revisited: A Conversation with Donald Campbell." *Evaluation* 1 (1973): 7-13.

Scriven, Michael. "The Methodology of Evaluation." In *Perspectives of Current Evaluation*. AERA Monograph Series on Methodology. Chicago: Rand McNally, 1967.

Taylor, James. "Introducing Social Innovations." *Journal of Applied Behavioral Sciences* 6 (1970): 69-77.

Thompson, James. *Organizations in Action*. New York: McGraw-Hill, 1967.

Tripodi, Tony; Fellini, Phillip; and Epstein, Irwin. *Social Program Evaluation*. Itasca, Ill.: Peacock, 1971.

Van den Ven, Andrew, and Delbecq, Andre L. "A Task Contingent Model of Work Unit Structure." *Administrative Science Quarterly* 19 (1974): 183-97.

Van den Ven, Andrew, and Koenig, Richard, Jr. "A Process Model for Program Planning and Evaluation." *Journal of Economics and Business* (1976): 161-70.

Yuchtman, Ephram, and Seashore, Stanley. "A System Resource Approach to Organizational Effectiveness." *American Sociological Review* 32 (1967): 891-903.

Zaltman, Gerald; Duncan, Robert; and Holbek, Jonny. *Innovations and Organizations*. New York: Riley, 1973.

MEASURING COMPETENCE IN SOCIAL WORK PRACTICE

Robert O. Washington

A fundamental premise of our democratic society has been that members of organizations, public or voluntary, entrusted with the authority to expand public resources have a responsibility to render a full accounting of their activities. This form of accounting, which is the backbone of our governmental process, has recently been extended to the field of social work. In social work programs, accountability of service delivery requires the specification not only of the goals to which public resources are devoted but also of the manner in which services are delivered and of their effects on clients.

Some observers believe that social work practice today is struggling with an accountability crisis. In assessing efforts to measure social work practice competence, Mullen has noted that, although a large number of outcome evaluations exist, "we have not had the wisdom, skill, or time to assess or integrate their meaning."[1] At the same time, there remains a paucity of data with which to judge the relative worth of different modes of intervention with respect to desired outcomes.

The problem of outcome data is only one dimension of the accountability crisis. The other is that because of an exponential growth in social problems, coupled with a diminishing supply of funds to deal with these problems, social workers must become more disciplined in their efforts to measure the competence of their work. They must begin to systematize their evaluation efforts to provide reliable and relevant information that can be used by decision makers in judging intervention effectiveness, alternative uses of funds, and whether certain interventions are cost-beneficial. In other words, social workers must perfect and standardize a set of evaluative research skills which will make it possible to do authoritative studies of the major issues confronting the profession and to answer the basic question: which intervention is effective under what conditions?

The purpose of this paper is to offer an analytical frame of reference for standardizing procedures for measuring social work competence. The proposition to be argued is that the lack of standardization creates ambiguity about outcomes, particularly in comparisons of the effectiveness of different modes of social work intervention. As a consequence, different evaluators studying the same phenomena will often obtain different findings. Moreover, without standardization it is difficult to determine whether the differences in findings on alternative modes of intervention reflect actual differences in outcomes or are the results of different measures. When measures are standardized, since one possible source of difference is controlled, the likelihood increases that findings reflect differences in intervention.

The proposition will be defended using a series of definitions and assumptions which may serve to circumscribe evaluation behavior and, at the same time, to suggest an evaluation paradigm consistent with social work values and practice.

DEFINITION OF EVALUATION

The first task is to establish a definition of evaluation. Evaluation is defined as the process of determining the success of a particular intervention in terms of costs and benefits and of goal attainment. It is concerned also with assessing the significance and relevance of the stated goal, the feasibility of attaining it, and the impact of unintended outcomes.

This conception of evaluation is used because it emphasizes the relationship between evaluation and decision making, particularly concerning the continuation, modification, expansion, or elimination of programs. The decision maker uses evaluation data to determine, first, whether or not a program was carried out in accordance with the prescriptions set forth in the planning and development stages, and second, to what degree impacts sought by the program have been achieved. Evaluation also is used in attempts to ascertain whether the expenditure of resources has been efficient in comparison with alternative means of achieving the same objective.

This definition informs the evaluator that his first task is to identify the goal(s) toward which the program or intervention is aimed. The evaluator often will discover that agency program goals are ill-defined. Moreover, the publicly stated goals may not be the ones which guide the agency's activities. The evaluator must therefore not only specify the goals to be measured but also frequently actively help the agency to identify and decide upon appropriate goals. Sometimes the evaluator must conduct a needs assessment to ascertain the degree to which goals respond to empirically established needs.

Another important feature of this definition is that it suggests that evaluation must include measures of input and process variables as well as output variables.

Input Evaluation

The measurement of input frequently referred to as program monitoring concerns the degree to which the actual program resembles the proposed program. This process also identifies program goals and independent variables (the ways in which goals are being implemented) and permits the comparison of baseline and post-intervention data.

Input variables include such factors as the identifying characteristics of those receiving the intervention or service; administrative resources; the amount of effort functionaries exert toward the achievement of program goals; the nature and demands of the program components; the inherent characteristics of functionaries which affect their ability to carry out certain policy goals; recipient demands and aspirations; and the debilitating and facilitating features of the social context in which the program is operative. All of these factors are important indicators of whether a program will reach its goal.

The rationale for the use of input measures is that program impact cannot be measured unless program compliance is measured first. Since the two fundamental tasks of evaluation are to measure the extent to which the program has achieved its predetermined goals and to demonstrate that program outcomes can be attributed to the implementation of program inputs, an evaluation design which does not include measures of input should be considered methodologically inadequate.

Input evaluation makes an important contribution to decisions about how resources should be used to attain program goals. It does so by: (1) identifying and appraising the potential of individuals and agencies; (2) comparing and analyzing possible strategies for achieving goals; (3) formulating designs for implementation; and (4) estimating immediate staff and other resource requirements and costs, as well as possible difficulties.

Process Evaluation

Process evaluation is an essential step in measuring social work competence because outcomes cannot be measured unless the process of implementation is understood.

Process variables include: physical facilities; services offered; staff attitudes and characteristics, including occupational training, demographic aspects, and behavior; administrative practices and policies; social norms; cultural ethos and other community attitudes and behavior; and facilitating and debilitating features of the environment.[2]

Measures of process seek to answer the question: what factors brought about change? They also provide data on the attributes of the program, the population exposed to it, the situational context within which the program takes place, and the effects the program produces.

Process evaluation allows program managers to review and possibly alter earlier decisions. It: (1) detects malfunctioning in procedures or their implementation; (2) identifies the sources of difficulty; (3) provides information for program revision and improvements; (4) appraises staff communication and adequacy of resources; (5) appraises site and facilities; and (6) projects additional resource requirements not originally anticipated.

Outcome Evaluation

Outcome (or output) evaluation is a measure of dependent variables representing the behavior the client is expected to demonstrate at the completion of the intervention. Outcome measurement involves: (1) identifying the correspondence of and the discrepancies between goals and attainments; and (2) identifying unintended results and suggesting possible causal factors.

Outcome evaluation seeks to measure change — i.e., progress in the direction of a social ideal — and the relationship between input and outcome. It also should provide data for: (1) determining whether to change previous planning, input, and process decisions; (2) providing quality control through recycling the program to attain unmet goals; and (3) deciding whether to continue, modify, or terminate the program.[3]

FORMULATING AN EVALUATION STRATEGY

Underlying the foregoing definition of evaluation is the assumption that the evaluator must not merely measure change but must assess the performance of the total system. Measuring change is a relatively straightforward matter of comparing initial with later measurements. The real problem is one of ascribing relative change to different interventions.

Design Criteria

Evaluation theorists argue that in order to conclude that a particular outcome resulted from a particular social work input certain minimal design criteria must be met: (1) there must be a control or comparison group; (2) there must be random assignment to both groups; and (3) timing and conditions of data collection must be the same for the two groups.

Figure 1 shows the basic paradigm by which these three criteria are achieved and to which most experimental designs conform. While many variations are possible, the logic remains fundamentally the same.

The diagram shows a target population selected for study and a sample taken from that population. The sample is divided into two groups by a method which assumes that the factors which might influence the results have at least a probable chance of occurring in both groups. Tests are given, or baseline measures taken, in both the experimental and the control groups, to ensure that the two groups are similar at the beginning of the study. If there are differences, they are known differences. One group then receives treatment, or program input, and the other does not. The measurements applied at the baseline are applied again after the "treatment" has had time to take effect. Three more comparisons are then made: (1) the experimental group is compared with itself before and after "treatment"; (2) the control group is compared with itself before and after the nontreatment period; and (3) the two comparisons are compared.

The evaluator should follow six basic steps in formulating an evaluation strategy. He should:

1. state the problem
2. select the standards or criteria against which judgments are to be made (what is hoped to be accomplished by the end of the project?)
3. identify the indicators which will permit measurement of the changes to be brought about
4. collect data on indicators, including baseline data if not already available
5. analyze data for: (a) rates of change; (b) direction of change; (c) nature of change; and (d) amount of change
6. interpret the data analysis in terms of the following questions: (a) was the predetermined goal met? (b) did the program activity make a significant impact on society in general? (c) was the impact worth the cost in effort, resources, and time? (d) what were the critical factors that determined the outcome?

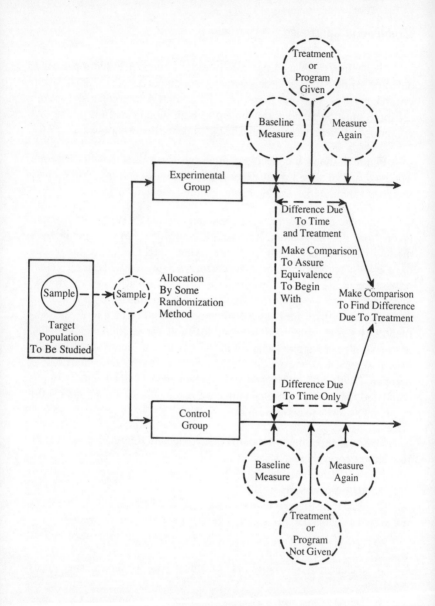

FIGURE 1
"Ideal" Study Design for Making Comparisons*

*Reprinted from *Evaluation Handbook,* Second Edition, Office of Program Evaluation, USAID, MC 1026.1 Supplement II, Washington, D.C. 20523.

Problems of Controlled Evaluations

This design is only a prototype and admittedly is not suitable for use in the evaluation of social work competence in every situation. In fact, in certain circumstances the use of controlled evaluation may create problems for both the evaluator and the social worker. First, selecting a comparison group which matches the treatment group in all respects except for the treatment is rarely if ever possible. Dymond[4] has argued that since a program usually is developed in response to the needs of a particular group of individuals in a particular setting, real functional differences exist between programs:

> *Only rarely are the objectives and clientele served by one program truly substitutable for another. . . . Once launched, programs tend to have an organic life of their own although time and circumstances render some of them obsolete.*

Second, many evaluators contend that, because of the difficulty in dealing with the complexities of human feelings and action, experimental methods alone are inadequate for measuring the effects of treatment-oriented programs. Related to this point is the fact that the use of experimental designs requires that treatment and control conditions be held constant throughout the period of the intervention. Experimental designs prevent rather than promote changes in the intervention, because once the intervention is in process it cannot be altered if the data on the differences it produces are to be unequivocal. In this sense, the application of experimental designs to the evaluation of social work competence conflicts with the concept that evaluation should facilitate decision making and, in turn, the continual improvement of service delivery. Dyer[5] has expressed the social work point of view with the following observation:

> *We evaluate, as best we can, each step of the program as we go along so that we can make needed changes if things are not turning out well. This view of evaluation may make some of the experimental design people uneasy because it seems to interfere with the textbook rules for running a controlled experiment. . . .*

In a true experimental evaluation, random assignment of subjects is based on the probability theory that each subject has an equal chance of being assigned to either the control or the treatment group. Clients with whom social workers deal are almost never assigned to services on this basis;

in fact, social workers who attempted to use such a practice would probably find themselves confronted with ethical problems.

A third difficulty is that much of social work practice is done in one-to-one situations — i.e., in clinical or therapeutic relationships. An evaluation of the effectiveness of this form of social work intervention is called a therapy outcome study. Such studies are used for single worker/ single client evaluations in which data are collected over a period of time and in which systematic manipulation of treatment conditions is part of the evaluation design. Therapy outcome studies incorporate such strategies as time series analysis, single case experimentation, $N = 1$ designs, etc., and are based largely on anecdotes and idiographic data. By employing pre- and post-treatment measurement, the subject is used as his own control, with the assumption that the behavior of the subject before the intervention is a measure of the performance that would have occurred if there had been no treatment.

Data Analysis

Once the evaluator has decided what to evaluate, he must then develop a "change" or "intervention" theory which identifies what constitutes the desired change as well as how it should be measured. In social work practice there are four generally accepted analytical frameworks for such a theory. They are the (1) goal-attainment; (2) impact; (3) systems; and (4) behavioral models of evaluation. Each framework represents a particular way of thinking about evaluation and defines evaluation questions to be asked.

The goal-attainment model asks the question: was the goal met? It usually employs ex post facto research design, relying principally on descriptive-inductive analysis. The impact model employs experimental design. It asks the question: what difference does the intervention make? and calls for the use of multivariate techniques. Such a "tough-minded" approach to human service program evaluation often results in both technical difficulties and intra-organizational friction.[6]

The systems model asks the question: how close is the organization's allocation of resources to an optimum distribution? This model presumes that some organizational goals are nonconsumer related and that certain resources must be devoted to system maintenance. The most popular analytical tool used by systems evaluators is the cost-benefit calculus.

The behavioral model of evaluation (B.M.E.) defines goals in terms of the outcome behavior of the clients. It asks the question: to what extent has the program intervention improved the client's ability to gain mastery over his environment? It employs the time series design, using the subject as his own control, as previously discussed. A major strength of the B.M.E. is that it requires the evaluator to consider the value orientations of three constituent groups — donor, service provider, and consumer — in defining program goals, and to hold the goals of the consumer to be as important as those of the service provider and the donor. Another strength is the model's assumption that a core function of human service programs is the reduction and eventual elimination of social and economic inequalities through redistribution of resources and of economic and social opportunities.

The nature and variety of social work practices necessitate the use of various strategies in evaluating social work competence. In most situations, the evaluator will need to select elements of several models in order to achieve a comprehensive evaluation strategy.

CONCLUSION

At this period of its professional life, social work practice finds itself caught up in an accountability crisis. The sources of this crisis are: (1) the inability to define social work goals in outcome terms; (2) the inability to adequately use research methodology for collecting data about comparative practice effectiveness; and (3) the lack of standardized evaluation procedures for obtaining decision-relevant data.

Since most social work efforts are devoted to directed social change, measures of social work competence must have the capacity to assess change. However, the evaluator must not merely measure change; he must seriously question the very premise on which a social intervention is based. Measures of social work competence must challenge all aspects of social work practice, as well as the organizational structure within which its services are provided.

FOOTNOTES

1. Edward J. Mullen, "Evaluation Research on the Effects of Professional Intervention," in *Transdisciplinary Issues in Social Welfare,* ed. Paul C. Vrooman (Kitchener, Ontario: Aimsworth Press, 1972), pp. 17-35.

2. D. Katz and R. L. Kahn, *The Social Psychology of Organizations* (New York: Wiley, 1966).

3. Paul L. Dressel, *Handbook of Academic Evaluation* (Washington, D.C.: Jossey-Bass, 1976).

4. William Dymond, "The Role of Benefit-Cost Analysis in Formulating Manpower Policies," in *Cost-Benefit Analysis of Manpower Policies,* ed. G. G. Somers and W. D. Wood (Kingston, Ontario: Queen's University, 1969).

5. Henry S. Dyer, "Overview of the Evaluation Process," in *On Evaluating Title I Programs* (Princeton, N.J.: ETS, 1966).

6. Robert S. Weiss and Martin Rein, "The Evaluation of Broad-Aim Programs: A Cautionary Case and a Moral," *Annals of the American Academy of Political Science* 385 (September 1969): 133-42.

REFERENCES

Dressel, Paul L. *Handbook of Academic Evaluation.* Washington, D.C.: Jossey-Bass, 1976.

Dyer, Henry S. "Overview of the Evaluation Process." In *On Evaluating Title I Programs.* Princeton, N.J.: ETS, 1966.

Dymond, William. "The Role of Benefit-Cost Analysis in Formulating Manpower Policies." In *Cost-Benefit Analysis of Manpower Policies.* Edited by G.G. Somers and W.D. Wood. Kingston, Ontario: Queen's University, 1969.

Katz, D., and Kahn, R.L. *The Social Psychology of Organizations.* New York: Wiley, 1966.

Mullen, Edward J. "Evaluation Research on the Effects of Professional Intervention." In *Transdisciplinary Issues in Social Welfare.* Edited by Paul C. Vrooman. Kitchener, Ontario: Aimsworth Press, 1972.

Office of Program Evaluation. *Evaluation Handbook*. 2nd ed. USAID MC 1026.1. Washington, D.C.

Washington, Robert O. *Program Evaluation in the Human Services*. Milwaukee: Center for Advanced Studies in Human Services, School of Social Welfare, The University of Wisconsin-Milwaukee, 1975.

Washington, Robert O. "Evaluation as Management Accountability." Paper presented at the 103rd Annual Forum of the National Conference on Social Welfare, Washington, D.C., June 13-17, 1976.

Washington, Robert O. "Alternative Frameworks for Program Evaluation." In *Tactics and Techniques of Community Practice*. Edited by Fred M. Cox *et al*. Itasca, Ill.: Peacock, 1977.

Washington, Robert O. "A Systems Approach to Program Evaluation." In *Gerontology in Higher Education: Perspectives and Issues*. Edited by Mildred M. Seltzer, Harvey Sterns, and Tom Hickey. Belmont, Calif.: Wadsworth Publishing Co., 1978.

Washington, Robert O., and Turner, John. "Evaluating Integrated Services Programs: A Case Study of the East Cleveland Project." In *Evaluation and Accountability In Human Service Programs*. Edited by William C. Sze and June G. Hopps. Cambridge, Mass.: Schenkman Publishing Co., Inc., 1974.

Weiss, Robert S., and Rein, Martin. "The Evaluation of Broad-Aim Programs: A Cautionary Case and a Moral." *Annals of the American Academy of Political Science* 385 (September 1969): 133-42.

PROPOSAL/PROGRAM EVALUATION IN FUNDING AGENCIES

Peter A. D'Agostino

The decision-making structure of funding organizations traditionally is composed of volunteer/staff committees recruited from the business and professional communities. Because these groups draw on a wide range of interests and expertise, their recommendations can be useful in both agency administration and the efficient provision of services. Members of these committees, however, frequently are faced with a frustrating lack of dependable information on which to base decisions. While it is relatively easy to determine whether a program is making efficient use of available resources, it is often much harder to decide whether a program is worth doing at all or, in the case of programs which are focused on the solution of the same problem, which one(s) to fund.

One source of the needed information is in the developing techniques of program evaluation, a branch of social science research whose purpose is to discover ways of describing the anticipated effects of programs and of measuring how well those effects have been produced. This paper offers a description of the basic steps of the evaluation process, along with a practical example of their application derived from the author's experiences in annual evaluations of a thirteen-agency inner-city youth development project over a four-year period for the United Community Services of Milwaukee.

The evaluation process can be used for assessment of both program proposals and program performance. The questions to be answered are essentially the same in both applications. The difference is one of timing — that is, before or after the program takes place. If evaluation is to be used as a tool for deciding whether a program is to be funded, program methods as well as the willingness of the proposing agency's staff to participate in and contribute to program evaluation will be key issues to be examined during the final decision for funding. If evaluation is to be used as a tool for measuring the performance of a program, methods, staff willingness, and staff success in delivering the program must be examined. Evaluation thus is not a static, time-bound research technique but a dynamic tool for both planning and allocating.

In practice, if done correctly, program evaluation is a natural extension of a proposal's evaluation plan. Although good proposals include good evaluative segments, unfortunately not all good programs provide for evaluation. The best and easiest place to work at the evaluative segments of a program is in the proposal phase.

EVALUATION STEPS

In approaching the problem of evaluating a proposal, the first step is to study the program definition. While this statement may seem unnecessary, experience has shown that it should never be assumed that such a definition exists: too many program-related activities have been developed simply because they "seemed like a good idea at the time" and have continued just because they have been done in the past. The program definition must answer the basic questions: *What* is the service? *Who* is to receive it, having what problems and traits? Who will deliver the service, and how many will be served? *How* is it to be delivered, and *when,* and *where?*

The second step in proposal evaluation is to determine the answer to the question: *Why* — that is, to determine the definition of the program's goal or goals. Starting with clear and accurate information from program personnel, the evaluator must develop a thorough understanding of these goals, which can then be transformed into propositions testable through objective measurement. These state that if people are treated in a certain way they will show certain predicted changes in their behaviors, such as increased occurrence of a desired behavior, reduced occurrence of an undesired one, or improvement in a specific test score. If the program personnel agree that changes in the behaviors listed are appropriate indicators of success of the program, the evaluator will be in a position to test whether the outcome occurs — that is, whether the program is having the desired effects.

The third step is to select the methods to be used in evaluating the program. Both program and evaluative workers must participate in this step because each group has unique information to contribute and because cooperation from each is necessary to the success of the study. A lack of understanding and agreement by either group will seriously undermine the quality and meaning of the results. The methods for testing outcomes as well as reasons for the choice of methods must be explained and descriptions given of the kind of information which must be gathered, how it is to be gathered, by whom, and in what order. When program staff are involved prior to program approval, the degree of their willingness to participate in the program's evaluation becomes clear.

The final step is the evaluation of the program itself. Data are gathered and analyzed: behaviors are counted and recorded, tests administered and scored, etc. At this time, questions can be answered about the program's accomplishments and about its actual (as compared to expected) effects, but only if the earlier steps have ensured that the data are both "clean" and pertinent.

APPLICATION OF EVALUATION STEPS

The example of the Youth Work Experience Program of the Inner-City Youth Serving Agencies of Milwaukee, Wisconsin, a collaborative effort involving thirteen inner-city agencies whose varied service programs all included work with disadvantaged young people, will be used to show how the steps listed can be used in practice.

The program was defined by the existing structure and clientele of the agencies:

What: The service was to be the provision of jobs plus employment counseling for young people.

Who: The target group was inner-city young people, ages fourteen to twenty-one, from low-income families. The service provision was to come from existing agency staffs, with each staff person supervising ten young people. The program was designed to serve 220 young people per year.

How and *Where:* The program involved the employment of young people in the other service-provision programs of the agencies, in positions such as teacher aide in day care programs, day camp counselor, recreation aide, and neighborhood organization aide. Supportive counseling was provided through weekly individual and group meetings at the agency with the agency supervisor and monthly meetings with the program evaluators.

When: The program itself was to be ongoing, but each young person was to spend approximately thirteen weeks in the program.

Why: The goal of the program was the admirable but somewhat vague one of "enhancing the development of young people ages fourteen to twenty-one." During a three-month series of discussions, program and evaluative workers refined this goal definition to include "improving understanding of self, increasing acceptance of self, lessening alienation of self from others, and enhancing vocational values and work attitudes." The formal objectives of the program were the attainment by the young people of post-program scores on certain psychometric instruments which would show statistically significant improvement over pre-program scores in these attitudes and personality traits.

Also discussed and decided upon in the pre-program (proposal) meetings were the methods to be used in evaluating the program. In addition to reducing the sense of threat and producing a positive attitude on the part of the program staff toward an evaluation process which they had helped design, this step ensured that the data would be gathered uniformly and appropriately as the program proceeded.

The program evaluation methods selected included a pre-test and a post-test of each young person, measuring the elements of the stated objectives (self-understanding, self-acceptance, alienation of self from others, vocational values, and work attitudes). [1] In addition, agency staff were to provide post-program narrative reports including: (1) subjective reports about the young people whom they had supervised; (2) feedback about the program; and (3) reports comparing the test scores with their own observations of the individuals on the same personality dimensions. The evaluation process thus had a built-in self-monitoring feature which would provide a warning if the instruments seemed to need revalidation. Additional program feedback was to be obtained through the evaluator's monthly meetings with the young people.

This material was then incorporated into the following year's proposal for participation in the program. Thus, each year's proposal was evaluated in the light of the performance on the previous year's program evaluation. This procedure was followed for the four years of the program, effectively using program evaluation as both a report on performance and a predictor of future success.

DISCUSSION

An evaluation project such as the one described here establishes a new base for the measurement of success. Instead of looking simply at the number of clients, at the dollars spent per client, or at the number of staff hours spent on activities whose impact on and value to clients are unknown, such a project asks what happens to people as a result of their participation in a program. As well as being useful to the individual client, data generated in such endeavors provide an invaluable base of information for ongoing program development, planning, and future proposal writing.

The full goal of evaluation is (or must become) the creation of better programs and the extension of our understanding of program results. The time is fast approaching when a lack of knowledge of a program's effect on people will be just as dangerous as an unsatisfactory outcome. When programs, goals, and objectives are clearly defined and outcomes reasonably predictable, the remaining task is to earn or keep the trust of the target group(s) so that a program can be carried out. Evaluation can and should play a vital part in providing the information needed for this activity as well.

Evaluation requires a commitment from both program personnel and evaluators to refrain from destructive behavior. Such behavior, as well as defensive/accusative attitudes, can be avoided if both groups believe that evaluation is a process not for extolling successes or pointing out mistakes but for enabling better services to be delivered to clients. Both program and evaluative personnel must be professional enough to work toward this goal rather than toward either uncritical system maintenance or system destruction.

In this paper a too academic approach has purposely been avoided in favor of an examination of the practical applications of evaluation. The view expressed that evaluation is both a proposal and a program assessment tool is based on ten years of practical experience with this method of evaluating. While it may not be the best method, it has worked and continues to do so.

FOOTNOTES

1. Details of the measuring instruments used may be obtained by writing to Dr. Peter A. D'Agostino, Graduate School of Social Work, University of Houston, Cullen Boulevard, Houston, Texas 77004.

EVALUATING CASH
WELFARE PROGRAMS

William D. Dawson

Over 20 billion dollars were spent on public cash welfare programs in the United States in 1977, over 33 million needy people were assisted by these payments, and approximately 342,000 people were employed in state and local public welfare activities.[1] It seems likely that programs of this kind and magnitude will continue to operate for many more years.

Given such projections, it is not surprising that there are many "publics" with legitimate concerns about public assistance. Their concerns are highly diverse and often intense. It is difficult for the legislative and executive branches of government and the various publics to reach a consensus on "what's wrong" and "what's right" with welfare. The publics expect simple answers to complex and massive problems and often lack access to relevant, reliable, factual information about both program content and program management performance. In such an atmosphere, myths thrive. Recipients, employees, and taxpayers give, receive, are influenced by, and act upon misinformation as well as facts about welfare.

In the presence of diverse and intense public opinion, government officials find it difficult to focus time and energy on solving the "most important" problems because concerned and influential people do not agree on what these problems are. There seems to be little agreement on what the welfare "product" is, what it should be, or how well it is or should be delivered.[2] With poorly focused objectives and with little harmony of effort among federal, state, and local levels, the system in many places remains in a state of static tension. Federal, state, and local legislators and executive branch managers advocate, develop, and implement competing agendas, which fuel the fires of controversy and contribute to the polarization of groups with competing values and limited facts. It seems that little effort is spent on identifying common grounds for concern or on developing common schemes for measuring the presence or absence of problems.

There are at least two major types of problems. One type is reflected in conflicts about federal, state, and local laws and regulations that determine who is eligible for what and in what amount. While skirmishes on these issues exist in the executive branch of government, most of the decisive battles are fought in the legislative branch.

Another type of problem concerns the quality of the line management processes that presume to cause lawfully intended benefits to be delivered to eligible persons. The executive branch typically has broad latitude in managing the delivery system for these benefits. Within this latitude, it is not uncommon to find serious delivery system deficiencies that have the net effect of modifying the "who gets what" limits intended by the legislative branch. As a result of management deficiencies in the delivery system, it is not unusual that eligible persons do not receive correct benefits or that benefits are provided to persons who are not eligible.

In income maintenance delivery organizations, quality of service and ranges of administrative costs vary widely. When brought to the attention of the public, the effects of management deficiencies in the executive branch generate pressures in the legislative branch. These pressures are often for additional constraints on eligibility criteria or payment levels, or for more expansive eligibility or benefit level provisions. Although substandard management practices, rather than eligibility and benefit conditions and amounts, are often the indirect cause of grant payment problems, they are not often the primary focus for pressures to change.

Because of the freedom for individual government units to practice, without broad public recognition, either relatively sound or relatively inept management of benefit payment systems, processes that compare management performance between jurisdictions should be encouraged. If fact can be isolated from fiction in measuring and comparing the performance of delivery systems, substantial improvements become more likely. Jurisdictions that do the "best" job of delivering benefits as intended by the legislative branch can be given recognition for doing so and can serve as administrative role models for less effective jurisdictions.

Program performance data now being collected by many government agencies show that it is reasonable to assume that real and substantial differences exist in the performance levels of welfare payment organizations. It is apparent that, given precisely the same laws and regulations, some organizations are much better able than others to carry out legislative and executive intent. In the light of recent system performance data, the argument that the laws and regulations are too complex to be administered effectively seems to evaporate. With reliable, valid, and objective performance standards and measurements, the performance of the "best" providers can be identified and need no longer be obscured by the performance of the "worst."

PERFORMANCE DIMENSIONS

The following criteria are suggested for judging the operating performance of units within a cash grant welfare system:

Performance Dimension I: "Effectiveness"

Public assistance programs should be managed in such a way that people receive exactly the legally intended payments and services for which they are eligible. If people receive payments and services as the law intends, the program can be considered effective. If people do not receive these payments and services in the amount intended by the law, the purpose of the program is not fulfilled and the program is to some degree ineffective. Government units must ensure that public assistance programs for which they are responsible are managed within acceptable tolerance levels of effectiveness. Credit should be given to units of government that achieve acceptable levels and corrective action taken to improve the performance of units operating outside these levels.

Performance Dimension II: "Equity"

Public assistance programs should be managed in such a way that payments and services are delivered with reasonable promptness and in a fair, nondiscriminatory manner. To the extent that payments and services are delivered effectively and in a prompt, fair, nondiscriminatory manner, the program may be said to be managed equitably. To the extent that some persons applying for or receiving benefits or services are discriminated for or against, or are not treated impartially in relation to other persons, or that benefits are unreasonably delayed, the program is being managed inequitably. Government units have a responsibility to ensure equitable program management within publicly acceptable tolerance levels and to take action to correct inequities. If the law builds inequities into a program, the legislative branch has a responsibility to consider changes in the law.

Performance Dimension III: "Efficiency"

Public assistance programs should be managed in such a way that legally intended payments and services are delivered at the lowest possible administrative cost. To the extent that payments and services are delivered effectively and equitably at a low administrative cost, the program can be considered efficient. To the extent that unnecessary public funds are expended in the process of operations, the program can be considered inefficient. It is not reasonable to expect the public to authorize unlimited administrative expenses to deliver payments or services. Government units have a responsibility to ensure efficient management of public assistance programs. Credit should be given to efficient operations and corrective actions should be taken where efficiency is not within publicly acceptable tolerance levels.

Thus, public assistance programs should be *effective* (cause people to receive the legally intended service or payment for which they are eligible), *equitable* (in a prompt, fair, nondiscriminatory manner), and *efficient* (at the lowest possible administrative cost). Achieving general consensus on these basic dimensions of program performance provides a basis for measuring and improving organizational performance.[3]

PERFORMANCE MEASUREMENT

Once the dimensions of performance are agreed upon, it is necessary to measure the performance of individual government units in order that the range of performance may be determined, tolerance levels set, and action taken to correct identified problems.

Effectiveness — Using techniques now being applied in some programs, it is possible to determine the extent to which individual government units are delivering precisely the correct welfare payment to eligible persons. The existing quality control process in the Aid to Families with Dependent Children Program (AFDC) has the capability to determine which state-level entities are relatively effective on this performance dimension and which are ineffective.[4] Judgment of performance is based on the extent to which errors are made in determining eligibility for public assistance and, if eligibility exists, in determining the amounts of grants.

In some programs and in some states, performance has for several years been measured accurately at organizational levels below the state level. Dramatic improvements have been made in many localities, while other localities continue to experience serious problems.[5] It seems clear from this experience that the level of effectiveness of a cash payment program can be both measured and improved. It seems clear also that, with continued concerted effort and using existing managerial techniques, the effectiveness of cash payment programs can be brought within publicly acceptable toler-ance levels. By monitoring performance on this dimension, federal, state, and local executive and legislative authorities should be able to determine how effectively the welfare payment product is being delivered at the national, state, county, or local office levels. It is possible to scrutinize this dimension and to decide at what point performance is within acceptable limits. It is also possible to identify problems more precisely and to quantify the impact of these problems so that agreement can be reached on which ones must be resolved first.

Equity — Performance on the equity dimension appears more elusive to measure than performance on either the effectiveness or the efficiency dimension. It is difficult to quantify in valid, reliable terms such elements as fairness, nondiscrimination, courtesy, kindness, dignity, and other traits reflective of a civilized public assistance program. It is, however, possible to quantify such factors as timeliness of service, results of fair hearings, access to immediate or emergency services, extent of underpayments, and im-proper denials of payments and services. It is also possible to monitor through the medium of questionnaires the extent to which clients and the general public perceive public assistance programs to be operating in an equitable fashion.

While much more work needs to be done on this dimension to develop both measurement and corrective action techniques, there appear to be no "state-of-the-art" problems to preclude precise identification of the exist-ence and the extent of equity problems on a system-wide as well as an individual government unit basis.[6] Once these problems are identified, the need for corrective actions will become more apparent. It seems likely that much highly polarized opinion and myth can be dealt with effectively if problems in this dimension are quantified. There is no apparent reason that "tolerance level" concepts cannot readily be developed to help identify problems and focus resouces on those most in need of correction.

Efficiency — Recent efforts by the California State Department of Social Services to control welfare administrative costs have provided an excellent base from which to move in measuring and comparing the effi-ciency of individual local government operations and in developing correc-tive action where problems exist. In conjunction with recently implemented cost control methods in several public assistance programs, new data are being collected and analyzed. Cost control limits or tolerance levels are being set and action is being taken to reduce costs where these tolerance levels are being exceeded.[7] Work measurement and systems analysis techniques are showing promise in dealing with identified problems.[8] The ability to contain costs within publicly acceptable tolerance levels by continuing to develop and apply administrative cost control devices appears to depend more on executive and legislative commitment than on managerial techniques.

RELATIONSHIPS AMONG PERFORMANCE DIMENSIONS

It is reasonable to assume that the three performance dimensions have a functional relationship. Many welfare payment organizations may be able to improve performance simultaneously on all three dimensions. A few organizations may be operating at an "improvement crossover point." In such organizations, demands for improved performance on one dimension may dictate degraded performance on one or both of the other two dimensions. Excessive administrative cost reductions may drive payment error rates up or level of service down. Extensive efforts to improve level of service may result in higher administrative costs or higher error rates. Overly ambitious efforts to reduce errors may drive up administrative costs and reduce the level of service. The impact of these relationships should be examined closely when legislative and executive branch policy options for both program content and management process are being considered. However, with adequate performance measurements it should be possible to determine where performance is susceptible to improvement without unacceptable adverse effects.

PERFORMANCE MODEL

Since it is assumed that individual governmental unit performance can be quantified on the dimensions described, it is theoretically possible to compare the performance of units within a three-dimensional model (see Figure 1). The performance of each government unit being compared will at any point in time be represented by a theoretical point in space in the model. Since it is assumed that tolerance levels can be established on all three dimensions, there will be a zone near the apex of the model where high performance units will be found. Units that are outside the tolerance levels on one or more of the performance criteria will be seen as isolates outside the tolerance zone.

Performance on any one of the three basic dimensions represents performance on many factors within each dimension. The overall administrative cost rating (efficiency) depends on staff costs, travel costs, space costs, purchased services, data processing, and other costs. Similarly, the

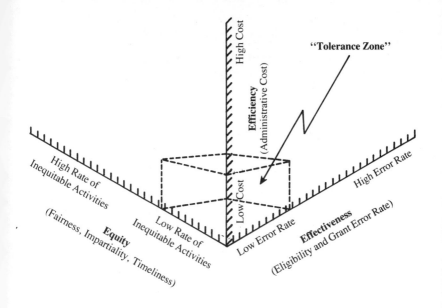

FIGURE 1
Public Assistance
Program Management Performance Model

rate of delivery of accurate grant payments includes rates of overpayments, of underpayments, and of payments to ineligible persons. Equitable service also contains a number of components. It therefore is necessary to determine not only whether overall performance on a dimension is adequate but also whether problems appear within components of the dimension. It is appropriate to determine also whether individual operating units have dominated the overall performance ratings.

Figure 2 can be used for locating performance isolates, whether among performance dimension components or among organizational sub-units. With government units to be compared listed on the left and the individual problem areas across the top, it may be determined whether a problem is broad-based (all units will have it) or localized (few will have it). The use of this kind of layout shows the source and extent of basic program management problems and makes possible the concentration of scarce resources on the solution of problems which most need attention. Equally important, it provides a simple way of showing that, relatively speaking, problems *do not* exist in some areas and that expenditure of resources there jeopardizes progress in areas in which change is needed more.

| Government Unit | \multicolumn{9}{c}{Effectiveness (or Equity or Efficiency) Problem Areas} | Sum of Problems |

Effectiveness (or Equity or Efficiency) Problem Areas

Government Unit	I	II	III	IV	V	VI	VII	VIII	XI	Sum of Problems
A	Performance Data									
B										
C										
D										
E										
F										
G										
Sum of Units	↓									

FIGURE 2
Performance Comparison Matrix

PROGRESS TRACKING

If performance has been adequately defined and regularly monitored, it should be possible using a graphic presentation to watch change occur over time (see Figure 3). Performance trends can then be evaluated and resources for corrective action concentrated in areas where adverse performance trends are observed. Such trend lines may be particularly useful for executive and legislative decision-making purposes.

SUMMARY

Massive amounts of public funds are being spent on programs to assist people who are unable to meet their basic needs independently. While the legislative branch of government has established conditions of eligibility and payment levels for welfare programs, the quality of performance of government units delivering these payments varies substantially. Poor performance contributes to dissatisfaction with the welfare system. If results-oriented, quantitative management performance criteria are established and used to measure the performance of welfare organizations, executive and legislative branch attention can be focused on the correction of many significant problems. The performance of individual welfare payment organizations can be measured and tracked on the dimensions of effectiveness, equity, and efficiency. Federal, state, and local quality control programs provide a data base for the "effectiveness" dimension and administrative cost data can be utilized to determine the "efficiency" of organizations. Better data management devices must be developed to adequately evaluate performance on "equity" or level of service factors. With reliable, valid, and regularly recurring measures of performance on the three dimensions, corrective action can be focused on significant problems, thus promoting the improvement of the overall performance of the system. Use of this three-dimensional management device at the state level in California has assisted in reducing erroneous grant payments, controlling administrative costs, ameliorating service to recipients, and improving the adverse image of public welfare programs.

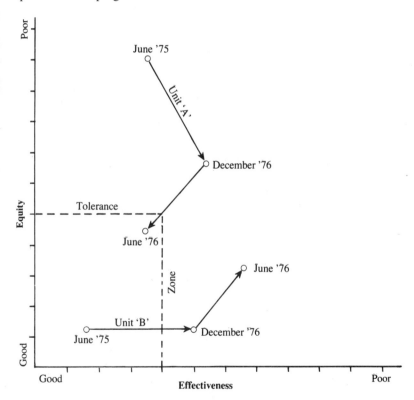

FIGURE 3
Performance Trend Chart

FOOTNOTES

1. Source: Data Management and Analysis Bureau, California State Department of Social Services, 744 "P" Street, Sacramento, California 95814.

2. For an example of the range of debate by members of Congress, public witnesses and administration witnesses about welfare reform, see the Congressional Record, Serial 95-47, 48, 49, 50; Administration's Welfare Reform Proposal, Joint Hearings Before the Welfare Reform Subcommittee of the Agriculture, Education and Labor, and Ways and Means Committees of the U.S. House of Representatives, 95th Congress, First Session on H.R. 9030 (1977).

3. Performance dimensions similar to those described here were tested in locations in California, Texas and Connecticut in a "Comprehensive Study of AFDC Administration and Management" completed in 1977 under contract from the Department of Health, Education, and Welfare by Booze, Allen and Hamilton Company, in conjunction with the California Department of Benefit Payments, the Connecticut Department of Social Services and the Texas Department of Human Resources.

4. The U.S. Department of Health, Education and Welfare publishes semi-annual summaries of AFDC payment error rates for all states. These summaries are available from the Director, Office of Quality Assurance, U.S. Department of Health, Education and Welfare, Washington, D.C. Individual error rates for California's largest counties are available from the California State Department of Social Services.

5. Progress in reducing California's AFDC payment error rates is discussed in biannual quality control — corrective action reports to the Federal Department of Health, Education and Welfare. Copies of the most recent California report are available from the AFDC Systems Bureau, California State Department of Social Services, 744 "P" Street, Sacramento, California 95814.

6. Information on developing quantitative measures of "equity" or level of service in California's AFDC Program is available from the AFDC Systems Bureau, California State Department of Social Services, 744 "P" Street, Sacramento, California 95814.

7. Progress in controlling AFDC administrative expenditures in California is documented in various reports available from the County Administrative Expense Control Bureau, California State Department of Social Services, 744 "P" Street, Sacramento, California 95814.

8. A May 23, 1977 "Evaluation of the San Diego County AFDC Program" performed by the San Diego County Office of Program Evaluation contains, in addition to other topics, a detailed work measurement oriented systems analysis of AFDC case management processes. Using this approach, the U.S. General Accounting Office in 1978 also completed a comprehensive study of Contra Costa County's AFDC procedures. Both studies are useful technical resource documents for increasing administrative efficiency.

AFTERWORD

When approaching the topic of administration, it is easy to focus on differences between organizations: the state of development of an organization, its profit or non-profit status, its available resources, the fiscal and legal requirements it must deal with, the people it serves, etc. In this period of scarce resources and financial constraints, however, instead of focusing on differences we must examine the common issues which administrators face. Because the same demands for accountability placed on human service administrators by California's Proposition 13 and by similar measures in other states are being faced today in industry, the following fundamental challenges to administrators apply to both industrial and human service organizations.

The first challenge is accepting and assigning accountability. Since administrators of human service organizations are asked by many different people to do things for many different reasons, conflicts and problems of limited resources arise. In attempting to meet this challenge, people in administration (as in other functions) have fragmented their particular responsibilities and have specialized. However, the changes brought about by Proposition 13 and similar measures have made such fragmentation very difficult. Administration must now step back and begin to look at who is accountable. How can accountability be defined and how can administration, which very often is reactive to needs, be moved to a proactive position from which it can begin to influence the decision-making processes in a human service or industrial organization? The response to the challenge of accepting and assigning accountability necessitates two fundamental qualities: courage and professional competence. These are needed because administrators have the burden of establishing priorities within the organization.

The second challenge is productizing services. To productize services, human service administrators must do what business managers are struggling to do, and that is to turn from a process approach and begin to focus on end products. What is the organization delivering? What is its mission? Only in answering these questions will managers begin to see opportunities for combining similar tasks that are presently being done in several different places. Thinking about outcomes forces administrators to take both a vertical (output) and a horizontal (process) look at what they are doing. They then begin to see whether there are some tradeoffs in what they do and how they do it. If an administrator looks at outcomes, such possibilities become much more apparent than if he or she looks only at process.

The third challenge is one of establishing performance measurements. Establishment of performance measurements is imperative in administration because in many cases the administrator faces multiple demands on available services and resources. The only way he can handle these demands efficiently is to begin to quantify what is available in terms of time, staff, funding, and other — more intangible — resources. This task is very difficult for administrators of human services because they are dealing with less tangible factors than those encountered, for instance, on a production line. Nevertheless, there is no part of administration that cannot be made tangible. The value of achieving such measurements is that the administrator can begin to communicate more effectively with clients and funding agencies.

The fourth challenge for administration is that of contributing to the planning process. Traditionally, the administrator has little time to participate in planning, and limited resources to optimize the time he has. Lack of involvement occurs precisely because he does not get information about new requirements, etc. enough in advance. In order to gain the lead time necessary to bring the best resources and the best talent available to bear on a problem, the administrator must become part of the planning process.

The fifth challenge is one of improving productivity. In the past, productivity (or organizational effectiveness) has had a quantitative orientation. Productivity has been thought to be concerned with cuts and losses — a negative connotation indeed. If administrators can become involved in planning in order that they know what is coming and how it will be dealt with, the productivity issue will become one of how to motivate people and how to change the reward/incentive system. The challenge of productivity, then, is to effectively utilize human potential as well as advances in technology and information processing.

The last challenge is one of coordinating approaches to problem solving in order to achieve organizational effectiveness. Meeting this challenge requires that individual managers adopt a broader view of problem solving by looking at who else is working on the same kinds of problems and by developing mechanisms for sharing information. In this way, administrators will begin to get the feedback they need, not only to help their operations but also to help one another.

These challenges must be met. The constraints that have emerged in the past two years are not going to diminish; on the contrary, they are going to increase. Thus, what administration is doing and the challenges it faces have far greater potential than is presently realized. Administrators of business and human service organizations will benefit from efforts to continue the dialogue begun at this important Conference.

Vincent Byrne
Director of Administration
Xerox Corporation

DIALOGUE BOOKS ®

A persistent and frustrating problem for both the human service professional and the advocate of social action is the fragmentation of information on important social issues. Most social science information is scattered throughout a vast publication system, impeding the development of effective approaches to social problems.

In order to counteract the effects of this fragmentation, DIALOGUE BOOKS bring together in an easily understandable style a wide range of opinion and information on timely and significant topics. By highlighting new approaches to problems within the context of existing interpretations of these problems, the DIALOGUE BOOKS series enables readers to stay in touch with developments in the social sciences. DIALOGUE BOOKS are based on an ongoing dialogue among people in these fields, a process which is essential if these publications are to remain current, relevant, and based on practical experience.

1978 DIALOGUE BOOKS

STRESS, DISTRESS, AND GROWTH $5.75
STRESS, DISTRESS, AND GROWTH: A STUDENT MANUAL $3.75
MORAL EDUCATION $5.75
MORAL EDUCATION: A CLASSROOM WORKBOOK $3.75
THE VALUE OF YOUTH $5.75
SCHOOL CRIME AND DISRUPTION $5.75

1979 DIALOGUE BOOKS

PARTNERSHIP IN RESEARCH $6.75
DELINQUENCY PREVENTION: EDUCATIONAL
   APPROACHES $6.75
DROPOUT $5.75
THE YOUNG ADULT OFFENDER $6.75
THE YOUNG ADULT OFFENDER:
   DATA MAPS AND USER'S GUIDE $20.00
MANAGING HUMAN SERVICES $6.75

DIALOGUE BOOKS are quality paperback editions.

Order these books through your local bookstore or through International Dialogue Press.

INTERNATIONAL DIALOGUE PRESS, P.O. Box 924,
Davis, California 95616

ACM-1

1 4 8 5 8   9